LAURENCE BROWN

Coins
Through the Ages

BONANZA BOOKS • New York

To
MY WIFE
for her help and encouragement

Acknowledgements

SEVERAL people have made suggestions during the compilation of this book and these I must thank collectively. More specifically I wish to record my thanks to Charles Wormser and John Ford of New York for reading through the North American section, my colleagues on the staff of B. A. Seaby Ltd, for checking various other parts of the manuscript and also A. Chesser for the loan of the Holey Dollar for photographing. The remaining illustrations are either by courtesy of B. A. Seaby Ltd, or have been specially photographed by Frank Purvey. American edition has been edited by Burton Hobson.

© Laurence Brown MCMLXI

This edition published by BONANZA BOOKS,
a division of Crown Publishers, Inc., by
arrangement with Sterling Publishing Co., Inc.
(A)

PRINTED IN THE U.S.A.

Contents

Introduction
1	First steps in collecting	13
2	Further points for collectors	21
3	Ancient coins	29
4	Europe I	42
5	Europe II	54
6	England I *Early Britain*	65
7	England II *Normans and Plantagenets*	73
8	England III *Tudors and Stuarts*	82
9	England IV *Hanover to House of Windsor*	93
10	Scotland and Ireland	100
11	North America	104
12	Canada	117
13	Central and South America	123
14	The West Indies	130
15	Africa	132
16	Asia	144
17	Australasia	154

Appendices:
A: Numismatic terms and abbreviations	159
B: British rulers and archbishops who issued coins	160
C: Latin legends on English coins	162
D: Latin legends and abbreviations	164
E: Mintmarks	166
F: Denominations of the world	172
Bibliography	177
Index	181

Introduction

SHOULD the question, 'Why do you collect coins?' be put to those who are already enthusiasts, many varied answers would be given. Some would say it is because of the fascination of handling an object that was in common usage, say, during the ministry of Our Lord, or owning a coin of Henry VIII that is inscribed 'h k' for Henry and Katherine of Aragon, whilst others would tell you that they must collect something and that coins give them the greatest satisfaction due to their artistic beauty.

Certainly there are many reasons for collecting coins and not the least of these is that if one is interested in collecting antiques, coins are the cheapest. It is a never-ending source of wonder to the uninitiated that many coins—particularly Roman—can be purchased for only a few cents each. It would be wrong, however, to give the impression that most coins can be bought for next to nothing; particularly fine specimens of some coins are priced at several dollars each, whilst others, being very rare, may run into hundreds of dollars, but providing you exercise good judgement and discrimination when buying, you can build up a worthwhile collection without spending a great deal of money and probably also make a good investment.

To most people, however, who are worthy of being called numismatists, for that is the name given to people who study the science of coins and medals, the thought of making any monetary gain out of their hobby is a secondary consideration. Numismatics is one of the most rewarding of sciences, and the more time one puts into studying it, the more rewarding it becomes.

The purpose of this book, therefore, is to indicate to those who think they may like to collect coins the best methods to adopt and to give some general overall picture of the development of coins in each continent set against the historical background. A volume of this size cannot attempt to give more than a broad outline of such a vast field and many details have of necessity been omitted; no one is more aware of their absence than the author. It can only be hoped then, that if one particular series seems to attract the reader more than any other, he will be prompted to delve deeper into the subject and consult more specialized and erudite works than this. To this end a list of the most useful reference works has been appended, bearing in mind their availability to collectors.

CHAPTER ONE

First steps in collecting

Forming the collection
There are many ways in which people become interested in coin collecting. Possibly you have been given an unusual coin in change, seen a friend's collection, or perhaps some interesting coin has caught your eye. Perhaps for some reason—possibly not entirely clear even to yourself—you have made your first purchase. Whatever the reason for your interest, certain facts must be borne in mind when you consider forming a collection.

First, perhaps the most difficult question of all—what to collect? It is impossible to over-emphasize the need for some basic plan; it is quite pointless to collect anything and everything that comes to hand. This only results in an accumulation of uninteresting pieces, most of which are in poor condition, and are, therefore, practically valueless. If possible, decide what to collect before you actually begin collecting, and build your collection in an intelligent, orderly manner. You will then not waste time and money on coins that later do not interest you, and it will prevent your ending up with a large quantity of coins that you will want to dispose of—coins which, in all probability, no one will want.

Many people begin collecting coins of their own country that they find in circulation or only those foreign coins available through friends or the foreign coin exchange section of banks. They can only decide on what to collect after obtaining a large quantity of specimens, finally finding that one denomination or one particular country interests them more than the others. If this is the case, at least try to collect only those specimens that are in extremely fine condition. Prepare a list of the coins that have been struck and check them off against this list as you acquire them.

A few words should be said at this point about the various ways in which you can collect coins. By far the most popular way is to specialize in one particular country or period of that country. Many collectors of American coins collect every issue of the modern series (about 1900 on). In this kind of collection, called 'series collecting', the goal is to find one coin of each date, from each different mint for the denomination you are interested in. One specimen of each issue constitutes a full set for any given series. Another popular method of collecting is gathering a 'type set' in which one coin serves to represent all the different issues of the same design or style, that is to say, of the same 'type'. This is an inexpensive way to collect the older issues since a type collector normally chooses one of the commoner dates of a series to represent the type and purchases it for a fraction of the price of the rarities.

Much the same is true for coins of other countries. Many collectors of English series collect all coins from Charles II to the present day, known as milled coins. The reign of Charles II is an important period in English numismatics since it was after the restoration of the monarchy that coins finally ceased to be made by hand, the new milled or machine-made coins replacing them. Others prefer to limit themselves to collecting only one denomination. Restricting the collection to this is, perhaps, one of the most convenient ways for the beginner to build up his collection as it is only a limited series, does not grow too quickly, and can be as complete as one cares to make it, depending on the amount of money available. As with American coins, if the money to be spent is only small, the collection can be restricted to only one coin of each main type, or if the amount is greater, one of each date.

To endeavour to collect one coin of each denomination of each date is a formidable task for all but a handful of the newest nations. Often a type set of pennies or comparable small denomination coin will give a representative picture of a nation's coinage. A collection of English pennies from Anglo-Saxon times to the present day provides examples of the early hand-made series with its highly individual style as well as the later more stylized coins of the milled series.

Specialization, however, does not necessarily mean that you have to collect only the coins of your own country or, say, English shillings from Charles II to the present day; why not coins with animals on them? Many coins show animals on them

FIRST STEPS IN COLLECTING

and a collection of these would run into several hundreds and could cost you as much, or as little, as you liked. A collection in which the coins are related to one another solely on the basis of design is known as a 'topical' collection. Weapons and coats of arms is another subject that lends itself to the coin collector; most types of arms can be found depicted on some coin or other, whether it be the chain mail that was used so extensively during the eleventh and twelfth centuries or the heavy 'Maximilian' plate so called because Maximilian, Emperor of the Holy Roman Empire, designed it: he is shown wearing an example on his coins. There are many other subjects, of course, that can be used as the theme of a topical collection.

Most coins, of course, have a portrait on the obverse (this is the side which has the most important design, the opposite being called the reverse) and if you are artistically minded a collection of pieces illustrating the various periods of art would be a most fascinating series to collect. Few people who have something of an eye for beauty can fail to be moved by some of the Greek coins, especially those struck *circa* 400 B.C. which is generally considered to be the finest period of Greek art. The coin illustrated on PLATE I, 4 is an excellent example of the heights to which Greek art soared and the crown of George V illustrated on PLATE IX, 5, compares but unfavourably with it. The two coins are poles apart when compared artistically and between them there are many coins illustrating, for example, the glories of the Italian Renaissance or the overcrowded and very ornate coins of the baroque period of German art.

Purchasing coins

Let us assume now that you are interested in American coins and that you have decided to limit yourself to collecting cents—one example of each type to begin with—from 1793 to the present day. How do you go about obtaining them? You could, of course find the Lincoln head types and possibly an Indian head in circulation but you could not obtain more than these from this source if you are only going to collect coins in extremely fine condition. It is certainly not worth collecting any but the very earliest types in anything less than this. Condition is all-important in numismatics and later on we will consider the intricacies of this, but meanwhile, where do you obtain your coins if not from circulation? The answer is, of course, from a firm of coin dealers or numismatists.

There is a very definite advantage in obtaining coins from these dealers as all their coins are guaranteed to be genuine and a reputable concern will unhesitatingly take back any piece should there be the slightest doubt cast upon its authenticity. Another advantage in working with a dealer is that you will not be overcharged. Too often the beginner buys a coin from a general antique dealer or jeweller who, being unaware of the true value of the coin he sells, thinks that because it is perhaps a hundred years old and in good condition, it must be worth a lot—and charges much more than it is really worth. Of course, it is possible to pick up a bargain but generally speaking it is better not to press your luck too far until you know what you are about. The names and addresses of the professional numismatists can be found in the classified telephone directory (yellow pages) under 'Coin Dealers'. All dealers, here and abroad, welcome inquiries and will be only too pleased to deal with your orders either through the mail or in their shops. A word of warning, however, is in order.

Most dealers have many thousands of coins and cannot show you everything. Do not go into a shop and say 'I would like to see some coins'. It is best to have some specific section in mind such as early date large cents or German talers before 1800, and then coin dealers will be only too pleased to show you what they have. Department store coin centres and coin shops usually have extensive displays of coins on view that are very interesting and instructive to the new collector. Coin dealers can be of assistance in many ways other than selling coins and are usually glad to offer helpful and knowledgeable suggestions regarding your collecting plans.

Coins can also be purchased at auction sales. In the United States, an auction sale is usually held in conjunction with conventions (of the American Numismatic Association, and others) and many club meetings. The larger of these have a printed catalogue available in advance from the auctioneer and bids can be entered by mail or from the floor. In England, most auctions are held by Messrs Glendinings in their rooms in Blenheim Street, London, but occasionally both Christie's and Sotheby's (London) also have coin sales. The items are usually on view before the sale and (in England) it is possible to leave your bid with the auctioneer who will execute your bids without charge or, if you prefer, one of the dealers will act on your behalf for a five per cent commission. If required the dealer will give you his opinion on authenticity and also suggest a valuation; no extra charge is made for this.

Many European coin dealers also hold auction sales and gladly accept mail bids. In some countries there is a sales tax that has to be paid in addition to the actual price realized; this varies between five and twelve and a half per cent. If you intend to bid personally at an auction sale, whether in this country or abroad, it is worth remembering that if you purchase the wrong lot by mistake, or bid higher than you intend, you are bound to accept it, and that in most cases you will be expected to collect your purchases and pay for them in full within at least two days of the conclusion of the sale.

State of preservation

As mentioned earlier, condition is an all-important factor in numismatics and since the price that you will be asked for a coin depends very largely upon its condition or state of preservation, it is necessary to appreciate fully the intricacies of this rather difficult subject. There is a very definite standard by which coins are judged and the terms used to describe condition are as follows:

Gem Uncirculated (or FDC—Fleur de coin): Perfect mint state.

Uncirculated (Unc.): In new condition but may show very slight signs of handling though not of wear.

Extremely fine (EF): Nearly as good as uncirculated. No definite signs of wear but the very highest points of the design may show the slightest signs of rubbing.

Very fine (VF): A definitely used coin but only the very slightest wear on high parts of the design.

Fine (F): Perceptible signs of wear, particularly on fine detail.

Very good (VG): Shows an appreciable amount of wear. A coin in this condition should be free of serious gouges or mutilations but may be somewhat scratched up from use.

Good (G): Shows a considerable amount of wear. Major portions of the design distinguishable still.

Fair: A very worn piece. May be bent or corroded as well.

Poor: An excessively worn and highly undesirable piece unless it is of the greatest rarity, in which case it may serve as a temporary space-filler.

The difference between FDC and Uncirculated is often confusing to the layman, but can be explained as follows: FDC, meaning perfect mint state, is a term which can only be applied to a coin that is in absolutely perfect condition, without any wear or scratches on it whatsoever. Owing to modern methods of minting, where coins move along conveyor belts, slide down chutes and are packed into bags, it is almost impossible to obtain a modern coin that has been subjected to this sort of treatment in anything like FDC condition. The term 'uncirculated' more accurately describes the condition of new, modern coins. This may sound confusing but you will learn by experience the finer points in grading coins and the cliché, 'practice makes perfect', has never been more true than in this case. A point worth remembering is that it is always better to under-describe a coin than to over-describe it.

The standards for rating coins are those in use by American collectors. English ratings of used coins tend to differ by a whole category, the standards for each grade being not quite so high. Thus a coin rated only 'fine' by an American collector might be judged 'very fine' by his English counterpart.

Rarity and prices

The second factor that has bearing on the value of a coin is its degree of rarity. Here again, there are two methods of classifying coins, the most usual being R = rare: RR = very rare: RRR = extremely rare: RRRR = highest rarity. The descriptions in continental catalogues sometimes do not abbreviate the terms but simply catalogue the item as 'sehr selten' or 'molto raro', when the English equivalent would read 'very rare'. The custom of using up to four R's is a well-tried system and is universally understood, but it does not, however, cater for the finer points of rarity. In consequence some reference books use a single R with a small number following it, indicating the degree of rarity. For example, some catalogues use R^7 for the rarest coins, while others may use R^{10} so if this method is encountered, it is necessary to look up the number used to indicate the rarest coins and thereby

FIRST STEPS IN COLLECTING 19

gain some idea of how the other numbers stand in relation to it.

The value of a coin, as indicated above, depends *not* on its age but on the state of preservation and in some instances in the case of Greek coins, the style of execution. Apart from these factors, the law of supply and demand also applies. Naturally if there were, say, five hundred specimens of a particular type coin struck and only five hundred collectors wanted them the value of the coin would be small but when the number increases and five thousand collectors want the same coin the price could be multiplied by at least ten times. Generally speaking, the 'very fine' price is double that of the 'fine', and the 'extremely fine' double that of the 'very fine': if the coin is *really* FDC with a lovely 'tone' on it, the price is at least double that of the 'extremely fine'. Certain coins, however, normally occur in very poor condition and pieces in exceptional state of preservation command a much higher price than the examples given above.

Cleaning coins

The toning or tarnishing of coins is an occurrence that often bothers collectors who are new to numismatics. As a rule, a coin that has an attractive tone on it is generally reckoned to be worth more than the coin that has not, and to attempt to remove this tone would almost certainly reduce the value of the coin. The shade of the tone is dependent upon the chemical composition of the atmosphere to which it has been exposed. Coins stored in industrial areas are more liable to tarnish than others, due no doubt to the high concentration of chemicals in the air. In many cases the tone appears on silver coins only around the lettering or the design, leaving the field (that part of the coin that has no design) quite free. This seems to indicate that the part of the coin that has been subject to the greatest stress in striking is more liable to tarnish than that which has not.

Silver coins tone the most readily while gold and copper are very much more reluctant. Gold coins, if they do tone, usually do so in various shades of red while some ancient copper coins, particularly Roman sestertii, take on a lovely green patina. On no account try to remove this as the coin would certainly be ruined during the process. There are some liquid coin cleaners on the market under various trade names that are fairly satisfactory for removing tarnish from modern, uncirculated copper coins. They work by chemical action and it is only necessary to dip the coin in the liquid and wash it off as per the manufacturer's instructions. For used copper coins, a little olive oil on a soft cloth can be used to remove most of the scum picked up in circulation.

All silver coins, particularly FDC or uncirculated pieces, tarnish in time—regardless of the steps you may take to prevent it. Modern silver coins respond to cleaning quite well and there are various brands of liquid cleaner as for the copper coins. On used silver coins, a paste of baking soda and water will effectively remove tarnish. Beware of too much rubbing as you do not want your coins to look obviously cleaned. Actually, the short answer to anyone who says 'How can I clean my coins?' is 'Don't.' The purpose of any cleaning should be to restore a coin as nearly as possible to its original appearance. Before attempting to clean a prized coin, it is best to practise on some coin that you do not value too highly.

After the preceding suggestions for removing the unsightly tarnish from coins a simple suggestion as to how to darken the coin down again might not come amiss. The easiest way is to leave the offending coin on the mantelpiece over a coal, or better still, a log fire for a few days; this should tone the coin down again to a more or less presentable shade.

Although the above suggestions for cleaning coins are successful in some cases I would repeat the warning given earlier: unless you know what you are about, don't do it. There is an adage in the coin business that is unfortunately only too true: more good coins have been ruined by cleaning than have been improved by it.

CHAPTER TWO

Further points for collectors

Housing the collection

Housing the coins is a problem that all collectors must face sooner or later and one that can be solved in a variety of ways. For United States coins an album of some type is generally used for housing and display. The newest style albums are in the shape of books. They have slots for each coin with transparent sliding covers which hold the coins in place while allowing complete visibility of both sides. For date and mint mark collections, each opening is imprinted with this information as well as the figure for the quantity struck. In forming a 'series' collection the collector attempts to find one coin of each issue and he tries to obtain it in the best possible condition. The sliding cover feature makes it possible to change coins readily when a specimen is found in superior condition.

There are also 'push-in' folders available for American, Canadian and some English coins. Some show both sides of the coins, others only the obverse. Because of the huge quantities produced they are all relatively inexpensive.

World-wide collections or others where the coins are not of uniform size are often written up and stored in special 2 in. × 2 in. coin envelopes. Pertinent data can be written right on the envelope and your information is always available with the coin. Coins stored in envelopes can be further protected by placing them first in cellophane inner envelopes designed for this purpose. Steel boxes can be used to store quantities of 2 in. × 2 in. coin envelopes and they have steel dividers to hold the coins firmly in place. The envelope system is perhaps the best for housing coins such as we will be discussing in this book. Serious collectors encounter many coins of irregular size and they, too, feel that merely pushing a coin into a slot to fill a gap is not numismatics although it is the usual and accepted way to start.

Coin cabinets are used by many collectors in England and on the Continent, and by many dealers everywhere. They utilize flat trays with round or rectangular divisions to hold the coins. A cabinet shows coins to good advantage and enables you to examine them very easily. Unfortunately, however, cabinets are expensive and not very portable.

The main object of any method of housing coins is obviously to prevent them from scratching against each other and to protect them from handling. Albums, envelopes or cabinets make it possible for you to keep your collection in an orderly, organized manner as well.

Clubs and societies

You will probably wish to discuss your hobby with other collectors and learn something about the coins other people are interested in. Since the addresses of the secretaries of local coin clubs change from time to time, we have made no attempt to list them but your local public library or coin dealer can very likely provide this information. Some of the more important societies are:

AMERICAN NUMISMATIC ASSOCIATION, Box 577, Wichita, Kansas.

AMERICAN NUMISMATIC SOCIETY, Broadway at 155th Street, New York 32, New York.

CANADIAN NUMISMATIC ASSOCIATION, 74 St Claire Street, St Claire Gardens, Ottawa 5, Ontario, Canada.

SOCIEDAD NUMISMATICA DE MEXICO, Venustiano Carranze Num. 69, Desp. 104, Mexico 1, D.F., Mexico.

BRITISH NUMISMATIC SOCIETY, c/o Dept. of Coins and Medals, British Museum, London, W.C.1.

ROYAL NUMISMATIC SOCIETY, c/o Dept. of Coins and Medals, British Museum, London, W.C.1.

AUSTRALIAN NUMISMATIC SOCIETY, Box 3644, GPO, Sydney, NSW, Australia.

Reproducing coins

Sooner or later the need for photographing or reproducing a coin by some other means will arise. Most sale catalogues of course illustrate the more valuable coins which are being offered and since the prime consideration of these photographs is to illustrate the condition of the coins, the photograph is usually made from a plaster cast which reflects an equal amount of light from every part of its surface. Photographing the actual coin is a much more difficult task since some parts of the coin are darker than others and reflect a different amount of light; to judge

FURTHER POINTS FOR COLLECTORS

exactly the right exposure is a problem which only experience in this particular medium can solve. The photographs throughout this book have been produced by this latter method and I personally feel that this type of photograph gives much more body and life to the picture than can be obtained from photographing a plaster cast. However, photographing the cast is perhaps best suited to the sale catalogue whilst the latter method is excellent for the text book. This is not the place for a long discourse on the type of camera required or the various lens apertures, lamp positions or exposures; suffice it to say that those coin collectors who are also camera enthusiasts will soon decide what will give the best results.

Plaster casts have been mentioned in the preceding paragraphs and a few words might be conveniently said at this point regarding the production of these. The need for a cast of some sort can be felt when either you wish to photograph the coin or send an illustration of a coin in your possession to someone else for comparative purposes. Only the finest plaster of Paris should be used, other plasters such as 'Alabastine' or 'Polyfilla' are not really suitable since their texture is not fine enough to penetrate into all the letters and delicate parts of the design.

Roll a ball of Plasticine in the palm of your hand to warm it and then flatten it on to a firm surface with a smooth piece of metal (a tobacco tin is ideal for this); dust the surface of the plasticine with a fine coating of talcum powder, blowing away any surplus. Press the coin to be cast firmly into the plasticine and build up the sides so that the cast will be reasonably thick, then turn the whole thing upside down and gently tap the plasticine. The coin, because of the talcum powder, will not be stuck to the Plasticine and will fall out. Make a thin paste of plaster of Paris and pour slowly and evenly into the mould, blowing the liquid into all the design. After a few hours the cast will be hard enough to prise the plasticine away from the plaster. Trim up the sides and back and leave to harden for a few hours longer.

A simpler method of reproducing a coin that is particularly useful when the coin is thin and rather fragile, is by making a rubbing. For this thin paper such as typing copy paper should be used. Hold the coin firmly beneath the paper and push the paper into the design with a rubber, then scribble over the whole coin with a soft pencil (2B is ideal). The result will be sufficiently clear for reference purposes and has the advantage of being much quicker than making a cast.

Coining techniques

Although in the succeeding chapters some mention will be made of the various coining techniques used in different eras, a short summary on coining methods in general will be of interest to those who have no knowledge as to how coins are made. As will be seen from the following chapter on ancient coins, the earliest form of struck coin (approximately 700 B.C.) was simply a bean-shaped piece of metal, either gold or silver, which was simply punched on one side with a number of squares. This very simple design of course needed no die cutting; all that was needed was a single square punch, which could be pushed into the coin as many times as required. Later on, when more elaborate designs were used and the coins had designs on both sides, a pair of dies was made by engraving and punching the design into them.

As we have seen earlier, the obverse is that side of the coin that bears the most important design such as the royal portrait and since this side would be more difficult to prepare it is generally assumed that the die with this design on it was the lower of the two dies where it would suffer much less wear and tear than the top one which was constantly being hit with a hammer. The lower die was set into an anvil or block of wood, the cast lump of metal placed on it and the top die, being held by a pair of tongs, would be hammered on to it. Coins are always struck cold nowadays and indeed they have been struck in this way for many hundreds of years, but owing to the thickness of many of the early Greek coins, these must have been struck whilst the metal was still hot and would flow easily into the design.

Not all coins were made by striking, however. Some of those issued by the Roman republic *circa* fourth century B.C., were cast by means of pouring the molten bronze into a mould and allowing it to cool. This method, one which was also used for the production of the early British tin coins, *circa* first century B.C. was not very satisfactory owing to the fact that it was impossible to reproduce the sharp detail of the design and this method was used but rarely.

Coins were struck by hand in England until 1561, when one

FURTHER POINTS FOR COLLECTORS

Eloye Mestrelle, formerly employed by the Paris mint, introduced his machinery for producing coins at the Tower Mint. The bars of metal were rolled and the blanks cut out by machinery driven by horses. The actual striking of the coins was also done by machinery but although the coins produced by this method between 1561 and 1571 were of a much finer workmanship, they were not popular and it was not until 1662 that machines became a permanent feature of the mint.

The first United States Mint was established in 1792 and coins struck in 1793. The original machinery was operated by horse-power and a single press working at full capacity could turn out a few thousand coins a day. A new Mint building was erected in 1816 but steam power was not introduced until 1836. Nowadays, with modern machinery, coins can be produced in staggering quantities, some two billion pieces being turned out every year. The Royal Mint in London produces nearly a billion coins annually for various countries and the quantity is growing every year.

The production of a coin from the stage where the artist's drawn design has been given approval is a lengthy one. The design is first prepared by artists in the form of a large plaster cast, some ten inches or so in diameter. A copy of this is made in metal and placed on a reducing machine. The surface of the metal of this so-called 'electro' is scanned by a tracer attached to one end of a bar. All the features of the design are accurately transmitted along this bar to a cutter. The cutter, moving over the surface of the electro produces an exact copy in relief of the design on a block of steel, in the size of the intended coin. The same design can thus be used for coins of different sizes. This is the master punch, and when completed, it is used to produce a 'matrix' from which a number of working punches are made. From these, the final working dies that strike the coins are obtained. By using duplicate punches instead of the original, the master punch is always kept intact—and the coins carry exactly the same design no matter for how many years the design is repeated. The date is usually added to the duplicate working punches only.

Coins are not struck from pure metals but from a combination of metals called an alloy. In the United States, the alloy currently being used for cents is 95 per cent copper combined with 5 per cent zinc; for silver coins the proportion is 90 per cent silver combined with 10 per cent copper. The various metals are melted into liquid in an electric furnace and thoroughly blended to make the alloy. They are then poured into moulds and allowed to cool, forming flat thin bars. After being assayed to confirm proper content, the bars are passed through a series of rollers to reduce them to the correct thickness for the coinage. Coinage blanks are now cut out of these flattened bars. The odd bits of metal left over are remelted and the process is started over again. After the cutting, the blanks are sent through an annealing furnace which softens the metal. In the process, the metal becomes stained so the blanks are washed in acid, followed by hot water, after which they are dried. In the next stage, the blanks pass through a milling machine which thickens the edge of the planchet and produces the raised rim that protects the design of the coin while in circulation.

The blanks are finally transferred to the coining machines: automatic, high-speed presses that can stamp out 10,000 coins an hour. The planchets are fed down chutes and pass one at a time into the space between the upper and lower dies. The dies come together with the blank sandwiched in between, both sides getting their impression at one time. By the action of striking, the metal is caused to flow into the design engraved on the dies and also into a collar which produces the reeding (or graining) on the edges of the larger coins. After striking, the coins are counted automatically and packed into bags that are stored, ready for delivery to the banks.

Forgeries

In the preceding paragraphs the production of a coin has been followed from its beginning as an artist's model until it lies in a bag awaiting distribution. At this point, therefore, it will not be out of place to consider how forgeries are made. There are three ways of producing a forgery:

(*a*) by making a cast in a mould from an original coin, or
(*b*) by making an electrotype, also from an original coin, or
(*c*) by engraving false dies and striking the forgery.

The form most frequently met with is (*a*). Fortunately, this type of forgery is perhaps the easiest to detect since, when

FURTHER POINTS FOR COLLECTORS 27

pouring the metal into the mould, it is practically impossible to avoid minute air bubbles becoming trapped in the letters and delicate parts of the design and these will invariably show up under a magnifying glass. The resulting surface also has a 'soapy' feeling which a struck coin does not possess. The pressure cast—a cast produced by forcing the metal into the mould by placing the two poles of an electro-magnet one on either side of the mould—is much more difficult to detect and a great deal of experience is required to spot forgeries made in this manner.

Forgeries that have been produced by an electrolytic process are somewhat easier to detect owing to the fact that they are produced in two halves, the impressions being filled with lead and then soldered together, an operation which invariably leaves a thin line around the edge. Electrotypes of the coins in the British Museum were at one time produced by Robert Ready for sale to schools, universities, museums, etc. Some examples of his work occasionally come on to the market but these can be identified by the letters R.R. or M.B. (Museum Britannicum) which are stamped into the edge.

The third method, the striking of coins from false dies, is the most difficult to detect if the forger really has a 'feeling' for the style which he is copying and executes an exact copy. One such expert was Carl Becker, a German, who produced some superb forgeries in this manner. As he struck these pieces from 1805 until he died in 1830, many of them have acquired through age a patina that makes them even more difficult to detect. Becker's skill extended over a variety of series from Roman coins to French medieval; fortunately, however, there is a book which was compiled by the late Sir George Hill containing illustrations of most of his forgeries, to which reference can be made before purchasing a suspected 'Becker'.

In recent years many more forgeries from fake dies have come on to the market, particularly in the American series of gold coins; these include one dollar pieces through to the big twenty dollars and special attention should be paid to this series before purchasing what seems to be a rare coin from any person other than a reputable dealer.

Restrikes, although not strictly speaking forgeries, are another trap into which the unwary may fall. A restrike is a piece that has been struck from the genuine original dies but at a much later date. These are fairly easy to distinguish providing one looks closely at the coin. Very often, owing to the lapse in time between the striking of the original coin and the restrike, the dies have become rusty and small raised spots will show up on the coin as a result; the field shows these marks particularly clearly. English copper coins of the reign of George III are notorious for restrikes, and very often the rust marks on the dies have been erased by 'tooling' them out with an engraving tool, a process which very often takes away part of the design as well, especially the more delicate parts, such as the stems of the berries in the olive branch held by the figure of Britannia on the reverse. Restrikes are usually worth less than the originals.

Summing up

We have seen already that there are many kinds of coins and different ways of collecting them. There are certain facts, however, applicable to all methods of collecting.

First, you must have a plan. Much wasted effort can be saved if you have a definite project in mind. Next is the concept of condition. The collector becomes much more discriminating as he progresses. If you try to acquire coins in choice condition from the beginning you will avoid disappointment later on. You must also choose a method of housing your collection. Coins that are kept in an orderly manner are easier to work with and show to their best advantage. Finally, you have been cautioned to know coins yourself or to acquire them from someone who does.

If you keep these basic rules in mind, you will spend many pleasant hours arranging and studying your coins and planning new acquisitions. At the same time you will become intimately familiar with and gain an insight into much of the world's history.

CHAPTER THREE

Ancient coins

Greek

Before coins were invented, trade was conducted by means of barter and it would have been up to the individuals concerned in the transaction to value one object in relation to another. Thus, three sheep were perhaps worth one bronze axe or one axe plus a supply of arrow heads. Obviously this system was unwieldy and the next stage of the development was for each area to decide on an object in common use in that area and relate all other objects to it. Since the communities living in those areas would have had different means of livelihood, some in northern Greece depending on cattle whilst others in Egypt and Mesopotamia were primarily traders using gold and silver, a variety of highly individual units of commerce were developed. The intermingling of traders from different areas again made a change necessary in the medium of exchange. It was, therefore, a considerable step forward when the third stage was evolved, that of stamping lumps of metal with a mark, thus guaranteeing them to be of a certain weight.

It is reasonably certain that the first coins were struck in Lydia in Asia Minor *circa* 700 B.C. by refugees from the city of Mycenae which had been overrun by their enemies. The earliest of these pieces were cast bean-shaped lumps of gold bearing a crude form of punch mark on one side whilst the other was blank. Unfortunately it is impossible to determine by whom the earliest coins were issued but it is more than probable that they were produced by merchants who crudely stamped the reverse guaranteeing its weight and thus obviating the necessity of weighing each piece again Not long afterwards the ruling authorities realized that it would be to their advantage to restrict the right to issue coins to. themselves, guaranteeing both the fineness of the gold and the weight of the pieces.

In order to identify the issuing authority it was necessary to place a mark on the coins that would make them instantly recognizable and in this way the great variety of badges that appear on Greek coins was born. The coin illustrated on PLATE I, 1, is one of the early pieces, struck in silver and issued by Croesus, king of Lydia (561–546 B.C.). The obverse depicts the heads of a lion and a bull facing each other; the reverse bears the simple indentation of a rectangular punch.

Many of the early coins were struck in electrum, a natural amalgam of gold and silver which was comparatively plentiful in Asia Minor, where it was washed down from the mountains by the rivers. This coining medium was, however, soon relinquished as the ratio of fineness between the two metals was not constant. A bi-metallic currency of gold and silver was therefore undertaken and due to the fact that both the Lydians and the Ionic Greeks were mercantile peoples who had enjoyed each other's friendship for some considerable time, it was not long before the Ionians began to issue their own coins based on the Lydian weight standard.

The island of Aegina, situated south of the port of Piraeus, was an important trading station and by the middle of the seventh century B.C. was issuing coins with its own badge, a sea turtle, on the obverse. The early coins usually have a reverse design composed of four separate squares punched into the flan (PLATE I, 3).

We have seen that each of the different areas had adopted their own units prior to the striking of coins and when they adopted the use of coins their types and weights remained individual. In the ancient world there were six principal weight standards on which the coinage was based; Attic, Aeginetic, Phoenician, Rhodian, Babylonic and Persic. It is interesting to note that these standards, as far as we can tell, seem to have derived originally from the Babylonian standard of the 'Manah', evidence of this being found when Sir Henry Layard conducted excavations at the site of Nineveh on behalf of the British Museum. During these excavations, Layard found a series of stone and bronze weights, the former in the shape of a duck and the latter in that of a lion. From inscriptions on these, mostly in cuneiform or cuneiform and Aramaic scripts, it is possible by various calculations to work out roughly the approximate weight of the various standards. Thus we find that the shekel was one sixtieth of a manah which in turn was equal to one sixtieth of a talent.

The drachm, a denomination common to all six standards, weighs 67·5 grains on the Attic; 97 gr. Aeginetic; 56 gr. Phoenician; 60 gr. Rhodian; 84 gr. Babylonic; 88 gr. Persic. The denominations in use at this time are listed below together with their relative values: some denominations do not occur in all standards, the fractions of the obol in particular only occurring at Athens.

Denomination	Value
Dekadrachm	10 drachms
Oktadrachm	8 ,,
Tetradrachm	4 ,,
Didrachm	2 ,,
Drachm	6 obols
Tetrobol	4 ,,
Triobol, or hemidrachm	3 ,, or ½ drachm
Diobol	2 ,,
Obol	⅙th drachm
Tritemorion	¾ obol
Hemiobol	½ ,,
Trihemitartemorion	⅜ ,,
Tetartemorion	¼ ,,
Hemitartemorion	⅛ ,,

From Lydia the use of coinage soon spread to other areas. Aegina, as we have already noted, was one of the first to produce coins and soon after, the district of Euboea followed suit, striking coins at Chalcis. The states of Athens and Corinth were also among the first to strike coins, the coinage of the former closely rivalling that of Aegina in popularity among the traders.

Early in the sixth century B.C. the design of the Athenian coinage was regularized and assumed for its type the head of Pallas Athena on the obverse and an owl on the reverse. Pallas Athena (known to the Romans as Minerva) was the goddess of wisdom and patroness of agriculture, industry and the arts; she was also thought to safeguard men in war. The owl was a bird sacred to her and was adopted as the badge of the city state of Athens. The coinage consisted very largely of silver tetradrachms which were commonly known as 'owls' for obvious reasons and since the coins were of such fine quality, they were readily acceptable to traders in all parts of the Greek world, remaining the principal currency until they were superseded by the coinage of Philip of Macedon *circa* 338 B.C.

It is interesting to note the style of these coins through the centuries for it gives us the opportunity to see some of the difficulties that the artist had to contend with when he cut the dies. On the early coins, both the owl and the head of Athena are crude. The profile of Athena is shown with the eye as viewed from the front and it was not until the early fourth century B.C. that it was discovered how to depict the eye correctly in profile. The helmet of Athena is plain until 490 B.C. when, to commemorate the Athenian victory of Marathon, decoration in the form of olive leaves was added to it (PLATE I, 2).

The coinage of Corinth is equally interesting and from an artistic point of view the early staters of the sixth century B.C. are of better style than either the Athenian or the Aeginetan of the same period. The obverse depicts the winged horse Pegasus walking to the left and the reverse a swastika pattern (PLATE I, 6). On later coins, the Pegasus type is retained for the obverse and is combined with a variety of reverse designs such as a Gorgon head or the head of Aphrodite—the goddess of love and beauty.

Cyrenaica adopted the use of coins at an early date and by the latter part of the sixth century B.C. they were being used in Macedon in Thrace. Persia adopted coinage about this period also, the earliest coins being of Darius I (521–485 B.C.). The coin illustrated on PLATE I, 8, is a silver siglos, the obverse of which depicts the king—probably Darius III (337–330 B.C.) in a kneeling running attitude holding a bow and spear. The reverse simply bears a rectangular indentation.

Some of the most beautiful coins in the whole of the Greek series emanate from the city of Syracuse. Large silver dekadrachms designed by Euainetos were struck between 406 and 400 B.C. and were intended as prizes at the victory games celebrating the defeat of the Athenian invasion of Sicily. The obverse bears the head of Persephone wearing a wreath of corn and drop earrings with four dolphins around her. The reverse depicts a quadriga or four-horse chariot galloping to the left with Nike the goddess of victory flying above crowning the charioteer. Below the chariot appear a helmet, breastplate and greaves representing the Athenian armour which was used as prizes in the games. The coin illustrated on PLATE I, 4, is a tetradrachm of a somewhat similar type by the same artist but without the armour or the artist's signature as is usual on the dekadrachms.

Many coins bear types that are connected with mythology; one such is the coin from Cnossus in Crete illustrated on PLATE I,

ANCIENT COINS

5, which depicts on the obverse the head of Zeus who was considered to be the father of both gods and men, whilst the reverse depicts a labyrinth. The story of the Minotaur that inhabited the labyrinth constructed by Daedalus and how it was slain by Theseus is too well known to be repeated here. The excavation at Cnossus by Sir Arthur Evans in the early part of this century produced much evidence of bull worship and the legend of the Minotaur may have arisen from the fact that captives were trained to clasp the bull by the horns and vault over its back—a feat which the Minoans themselves loved to watch and to practise.

An unusual type that is worthy of mention are those coins that were struck at Metapontum and a number of other cities where the design was in relief on one side and incuse on the other. The coins of Metapontum produced by this method invariably have only a single design, but the cities of Croton and Sybaris produced a curious joint coinage, which depicts a tripod in relief on one side and a bull with its head looking back, incuse, on the other. Probably, since the names of both cities are inscribed on these coins, they were intended for trade between the two cities.

The rise of Macedon as the premier power in the Greek world has already been mentioned and the capture of the town of Crenides on the mainland by Philip II gave him possession of some of the richest goldmines in Europe. The town of Crenides was renamed Philippi and from the gold mined there Philip struck large quantities of staters—commonly known as Philippeioi —which circulated over the whole of the then known world subsequently becoming the prototype for many of the coins of the Gaulish and British tribes (PLATE VI, 2).

If Macedon was a power to be reckoned with under Philip II, she was even greater under his son Alexander the Great, whose genius as a military commander enabled him to conquer the Persians, free Egypt from their yoke and invade India, where he proceeded to establish Greek colonies. Throughout his vast empire, Alexander established a large number of mints, particularly in Babylon where the head of Herakles depicted on the coins frequently bears a marked similarity to Alexander himself.

On the death of Alexander in 323 B.C. the empire, which he had held together by his dynamic personality, was broken up and divided amongst his generals. A considerable portion of the eastern part of the empire passed into the hands of his general Antigonus whilst Seleucus, a cavalry officer in Alexander's army, obtained Babylon. Gradually, continued dissension broke up the empire still further and Macedon herself in 148 B.C. finally capitulated to the Romans who by this time had attained considerable importance. From this date on, Macedon was no more than a province of the Roman Empire.

Roman

Until roughly the third century B.C. the Romans, in common with other Italian peoples, had used as an improvement on the system of barter, large pieces of bronze known as Aes rude and Aes grave. The latter were divided into several denominations, the largest—the *as*—bearing the head of Janus on the obverse and the prow of a ship on the reverse. By the third century B.C., however, increased trade with Greece made it necessary for the Romans to develop a coinage of their own based on the Greek weight system and to this end a series of silver coins was issued. One of the earliest of these depicts the bearded head of Mars wearing a Corinthian helmet on the obverse whilst the reverse has a design bearing a striking resemblance to that of a tetradrachm of Carthage struck some hundred years earlier.

Although it may be said that these early coins were influenced by Greek art the piece described above is an unusual coin and the new silver coins were definitely Roman in style. Many of them bear either the head of Mars or Janus on the obverse combined with a variety of reverse designs. A more uniform type for the coinage was introduced *circa* 187 B.C. when the obverse design becomes almost invariably the head of Roma the goddess who personified the city. The reverse design was also subject to less variation; the usual type depicted Castor and Pollux—the heavenly twins who were commonly known as the Dioscuri and were stated by Homer to be the sons of Zeus—riding into battle with couched lances. The word ROMA is usually placed below the horses' hooves on the reverse. On the obverse is a Roman numeral indicating the value, either X or V standing for 10 or 5 'asses'. The as, formerly a copper coin of the aes grave series weighing one pound was reduced to weigh only an ounce with the silver coinage valued in relation to it. Thus, the *denarius*, as the new silver coin was called, weighed some sixty-five grains and was equal in value to ten ounces of copper; the *quinarius* equalled five ounces.

The denarius and its half, the quinarius, were not the only denominations to be struck during the Republican period; gold coins as well as copper were also struck in varying quantities.

During the second century B.C. the power of Rome greatly increased and this factor, together with a rapidly expanding economy, necessitated the issue of many more coins. It was reasonable, therefore, that the authorities should wish to distinguish between one issue and another and for this reason a variety of marks such as a crescent, club, or an ear of corn were placed on the coins. A natural development from this was that the mintmasters, who were drawn from the aristocracy, should place their names upon the coins. They also varied the designs in order to extol the achievements of their ancestors and to remind the populace of certain events with which members of their family had been connected. Some of the commonest of these coins are those of Lucius Calpurnius Piso Frugi (generally abbreviated to Calpurnia) which commemorate the games of Ludi Apollinares which were established in 212 B.C. by an ancestor of the mintmaster. Another coin, almost as common as those of Calpurnia, is of Lucius Cassius Longinus which makes reference to a method of voting (the Lex Cassia Tabellaria) which had been proposed by his ancestor Lucius Cassius Ravilla in 137 B.C.

Throughout the period of the Roman Republic several hundred different types were used commemorating past people and events so that it is impossible to quote more than the two above examples. However, it is possible to generalize inasmuch as the obverse usually portrays a head—often that of Roma, Mars, Bacchus or one of the many gods and goddesses—whilst the reverse bears that design that makes reference to the event to be remembered.

Rome, at this time, was governed by a republican method in which the power was divided between the Senate, whose three hundred members were elected from comparatively few of the aristocratic families, and the Assembly comprising the more educated members of the public. The Senate also provided candidates for the two annually elected posts of Consul.

Pompey (Cnaeus Pompeius), on his return from his African campaigns whereat he had earned the title of 'Magnus', formed with Julius Caesar and Crassus, an aristocrat of extreme wealth, what is known as the First Triumvirate. That same year (59 B.C.) Caesar was elected Consul. Five years later Pompey was the only one of the three to be elected Consul and from this date the government was virtually in his hands alone, although theoretically the republic still remained in existence and the Senate wielded some measure of authority.

Coins in gold, silver and copper were struck by Pompey, but only in three denominations—the aureus, denarius (PLATE II, 2) and as. These coins struck during his lifetime depict, on the obverse of the aureus, the head of Africa with MAGNUS behind it whilst the as bears the head of Janus and reads MAGN. The denarius has some twenty-one varieties of obverse type and legend, but those that bear his portrait were struck by his sons after his murder in 48 B.C.

Caesar, who succeeded Pompey, struck denarii with a large variety of types, but it was not until 44 B.C., the year of his murder, that he received permission from the Senate to place his portrait on the coinage (PLATE II, 4). The aureus, denarius and sestertius were also struck by Caesar together with the copper 'as', the latter bearing the bust of Victory.

The subsequent period of civil war between Antony, who attempted to succeed Caesar, and the Senate as represented by Brutus and Cassius, is well known. Coins exist both of Brutus and Cassius as well as Octavian, the nephew and heir of Caesar who allied himself with Antony against the Senate. The defeat of the Republican forces at Philippi in 42 B.C., followed by the suicides of Brutus and Cassius, put an end to any vestiges of the Republic that had remained after the death of Caesar. In the months that followed, Antony, Octavian and Lepidus, who had succeeded Caesar as Pontifex Maximus (Chief Priest), formed the Second Triumvirate and executed some two thousand of their opponents together with three hundred senators.

Rivalry between Antony, who held the east, and Octavian, who held most of the western empire, led to rather strained relations between them, their quarrels being temporarily patched up at the Treaty of Brundisium in 40 B.C. In 36 B.C. Octavian took control of the legions under the command of Lepidus, who then retired into private life. Relations between Octavian and Antony

ANCIENT COINS

continued to deteriorate until finally in 32 B.C. Octavian prevailed upon the Senate to deprive Antony of his authority as one of the Triumvirate. This was immediately followed by a declaration of war on the pretext of Antony's associations with Cleopatra who, it was asserted, was causing Antony to neglect the interests of Rome. Following their defeat in the naval battle of Actium in 31 B.C., Antony and Cleopatra retired to Egypt where, by their suicide, they gave Octavian undisputed mastery of the Roman world.

Octavian received the title of Emperor in 29 B.C. and that of Augustus, by which he is more generally known, two years later. With the reign of Augustus there begins the long series of Imperial coins with the more regularized types. Some denominations which previously had only been struck occasionally were now issued regularly; gold coins became an accepted part of the coinage which was reorganized by Augustus. Although the relative values between the denominations were altered during the later years of the Empire, the following table will serve as a guide:

Denomination	*Value*
Aureus (gold)	25 denarii
Quinarius (gold)	12½ ,,
Denarius (silver)	16 asses
Quinarius (silver)	8 ,,
Sestertius (orichalcum, yellow bronze)	4 ,,
Dupondius (,, ,, ,,)	2 ,,
As (copper)	4 quadrantes
Semis (orichalcum)	2 ,,
Quadrans (,,)	¼ as

In addition to the above, one might also include the antoninianus, a base silver piece, which superseded the denarius, which had itself become very base, towards the middle of the third century A.D. In weight, the antoninianus was one and a half times that of the denarius but in fact it circulated at the equivalent of two denarii.

The antoninianus became more and more debased until, during the great crisis which followed the capture of the emperor Valerian in A.D. 260 it was reduced to a mere bronze piece with a thin coating of silver. The coinage was now in a chaotic state, with the worthless antoninianus being the only coin issued in any quantity. There was no silver currency at all and gold was only struck to pay the troops. The normal brass and copper denominations ceased to be issued. Aurelian (A.D. 270–75) tried to ease the situation but it was left to Diocletian (A.D. 284–304) to institute a complete reform.

Thus in A.D. 296 as part of his empire-wide reforms, Diocletian re-established a pure coinage of reliable denominations in both gold and silver. A new bronze piece with a silver wash, the follis, was introduced and the relationships between the new coins were: 1 gold aureus = 20 silver argentei = 40 folles.

The follis soon declined both in weight and size and in A.D. 312 Constantine the Great reorganized the coinage once more, the new system being based on the gold solidus of which seventy-two were coined from a pound of gold and the silver siliqua, rated at twenty-four to the solidus. Other denominations struck during later reigns include the silver miliarense (14 to the solidus) and the fractions in gold of the solidus, the semissis (half) and the tremissis (third). The bronze coins continued to decline in weight and size, and as nothing is known of their equivalent values or denominations, they are known today only by their respective sizes, i.e., Æ1, Æ2, Æ3, or Æ4; the largest being Æ1. Several attempts were made to halt the decline in the bronze coinage, notably by Constantius II and Constans who introduced the centenionalis in A.D. 346 and by Magnetius, who struck his large Æ1 (*pecunia maiorina*) in A.D. 352–3. Julian II (A.D. 360–3) struck a similar piece, but he was the last emperor to issue large bronzes in any quantity.

The bust of the emperor (or empress) on the obverse is a feature common to practically all the coins of the empire. The bust is surrounded by his titles, for example on some of the denarii issued by Vespasian (A.D. 69–79) the obverse legend reads IMP. CAESAR.VESPAS.AVG.COS.III.TR.P.PP. a literal translation of which reads 'Imperator, Caesar, Vespasian Augustus, Consul three times, Tribunica Potestate, Pater Patriae'. The title Imperator is that of Commander-in-Chief of the forces whilst Caesar is now taken as a title as is also Augustus. The practice of indicating the number of times that the emperor had been elected Consul together with the number of times that he had held the title of Tribunica Potestate—being invested with Tribunican power—is a means of dating the coin to a particular year. Pater Patriae

ANCIENT COINS

signifies the title of Father of the Fatherland. Some of the legends include the letters P.M., an abbreviation for Pontifex Maximus. It was also the practice to include in these titles some reference to military victories, thus occasionally we find legends including the following titles found on coins of Trajan (A.D. 98–118) GER (GERMANICVS), DAC (DACICVS), and PAR (PARTHICVS). The victories over the Dacians were particularly profitable, the spoils amounting to five million pounds weight of gold and ten million pounds of silver.

During the third and fourth centuries the emperor's titles were abbreviated somewhat. His titles Imperator and Caesar still occur, but instead of the lengthy titles following his name we find such titles as P (Pius—dutiful); F (Felix—favoured by fortune) and D.N. (Dominus Noster—our master).

The number of different reverse types used on the Imperial coins is vast, to say the least. Many of the Roman gods and goddesses are depicted with appropriate legends; other types are indicative of victories and the extent of the Roman possessions. PLATE II, 1, illustrates a sestertius of Antoninus Pius with the personification of Britannia on the reverse commemorating military successes against the natives following the construction of the Antonine Wall from the Forth to the Clyde. The letters S.C. (Senatus Consulto) beneath Britannia denote that the coin was struck by the authority of the Senate, as were all base metal coins up to the time of Gallienus (A.D. 253–68). This authority, however, was purely theoretical, the emperor being in effect the sole authority in the matter of coinage.

The Emperor Tiberius (A.D. 14–37) is worthy of individual mention since it is to his coins that the following well-known passage in the Bible refers:

'Show me the tribute money. And they brought unto him a penny. And he saith unto them, whose is this image and superscription? They say unto him Caesar's. Then saith he unto them, Render therefore unto Caesar the things which are Caesar's and unto God the things that are God's.'

Matt. xxii, 19–21.

This is a reference to the tribute or tax that was imposed upon Judæa when it became a province of the Roman empire in A.D. 6.

The tax was levied upon all males between the ages of fourteen and sixty-five and all females between twelve and sixty-five, the tax being payable in Roman coin. For this reason the denarius, to which the word penny is applied in the biblical translation, is known as the Tribute penny and although they are common enough coins, they are somewhat difficult to obtain, due mainly to the reluctance of collectors to part with them. An illustration of one of these coins is to be found on PLATE II, 5.

Following the banishment of Herod Archelaus in A.D. 6 the Palestinian provinces of Judæa, Samaria and Idumæa were administered for Rome by procurators or governors. They were given the privilege of striking small copper coins bearing the emperor's name and not the least memorable of the procurators was Pontius Pilate, whose coins are eagerly sought by collectors.

The shekel, a well-known biblical coin, is now a rarity, those struck during the second revolt of the Jews under Simon Barcochba being perhaps slightly commoner than those of the first revolt. Shekels of the first revolt (A.D. 60–70) bear a chalice on the obverse with the denomination in Hebrew and on the reverse a branch with three buds and 'Jerusalem the Holy'; half-shekels were also struck. The second revolt shekel depicts the Screen of the Tabernacle with the Ark of the Covenant and the Hebrew inscription 'Simeon'; the reverse bears the inscription 'Deliverance of Jerusalem' together with a bundle of twigs and a citron. A typical copper coin of the second revolt (PLATE II, 6) depicts a vine leaf with 'Second year of the Deliverance of Israel' and on the reverse a palm-tree with 'Simeon'.

Unfortunately, space does not permit more than a brief glance at this fascinating series, but from the foregoing it will be seen that a collection of coins connected with Christianity is of very real interest.

The Roman empire during the third century A.D. was the victim of civil wars and an ever-increasing number of invasions by barbarians. These attacks finally forced Constantine the Great to transfer the capital from Rome to Byzantium, renaming it Constantinople. It was also Constantine who adopted Christianity as the state religion, he himself being baptized on his death bed.

The Byzantine empire, which was to last for over a thousand

years, provides us with many interesting coins. To do them justice would take more space than is available; suffice it to say that this series should not be neglected because of its complexity; the coins are well worth a detailed study, if only for the wealth of interesting portraiture, the principal figures being those of Christ and the emperor. An illustration of one of the late copper coins depicting the bust of Christ is shown on PLATE II, 7.

CHAPTER FOUR

Europe I

France

Following the fall of the Roman empire in the west in A.D. 476, the barbarians spread over western Europe and proceeded to adopt the Roman system of currency. The solidus, a gold coin derived from the earlier Roman aureus, was the basis for their coinage and many tribes such as the Ostrogoths, Lombards and Merovingians made copies of these coins. During the seventh century supplies of gold in Europe became short and it became necessary to debase the gold coinage by the addition of silver, the Merovingians in particular striking silver in addition to gold coins. These silver coins, known as sceats, are of a small, rather dumpy appearance and weigh some twenty grains, their designs being derived from Roman coin types.

The Merovingian dynasty, descended from the Frankish king Merovech, was succeeded by the Carolingian and it was Pepin I (752–68) who introduced a coin quite different from the sceats; the *Novus Denarius* or new denier. This was on a thinner flan and formed a prototype for the deniers and silver pennies that subsequently circulated in Europe and finally in England. By 814, on the death of Charlemagne, the Carolingian empire extended from the Bay of Biscay in the west to Bavaria and Carinthia in the east and from the channel coast down to the borders of Spain and some miles south of Rome.

Charlemagne struck a very limited number of gold solidii at his mint at Uzès in Provence and Louis le Debonnaire also struck solidii at Aachen. The latter were the last gold coins to be struck in Europe until Friedrich II (1197–1250) struck his gold *Augustale*. Silver deniers and oboles were virtually the only coins struck by the Carolingians and by far the commonest deniers were those of Louis le Debonnaire (814–40) and Charles le Chauve (840–77). The obverse is usually devoted to a single central cross surrounded by the king's name, thus the coins of Louis read HLVDOVVICVS IMP; the reverse has a similar design with the name of the mint town around it, i.e. METALLVM (Melle).

KEY TO PLATES

PLATE I - GREEK

1 LYDIA
Time of Croesus, 561–546 B.C. Silver stater (double siglos). Heads of lion and bull facing. *Rev.* Two incuse rectangles.

2 ATTICA, Athens
c. 478–430 B.C. Silver tetradrachm. Head of Pallas Athena. *Rev.* Owl.

3 AEGINA
c. 480–431 B.C. Silver stater. Turtle. *Rev.* Incuse square divided by bands into five compartments.

4 SICILY, Syracuse
Agathocles, first coinage, 317–310 B.C. Silver tetradrachm. Head of Persephone left with three dolphins around. *Rev.* Quadriga galloping left: triquetta of legs above.

5 CRETE, Cnossus
c. 200–67 B.C. Silver tetradrachm. Head of Zeus left. *Rev.* Labyrinth.

6 CORINTH
c. 600–500 B.C. Silver stater. Pegasus with bridle walking to left. *Rev.* Quadripartite incuse in swastika form.

7 TARENTUM
c. 281–272 B.C. Silver didrachm. The Dioskouroi galloping left. *Rev.* Taras holding figure of Nike in left hand astride a dolphin.

8 PERSIA
? Darius III, 337–330 B.C. silver siglos. King to right in kneeling running attitude holding spear. *Rev.* Oblong incuse.

9 LOCRI, Locri Opuntii
c. 369–338 B.C. Silver stater. Head of Persephone left. *Rev.* Ajax holding shield and sword.

PLATE II - ROMAN

1 ANTONINVS PIVS
A.D. 138–61 Copper sestertius. Head of emperor, right. *Rev.* Britannia seated on rock. BRITANNIA, around.

2 POMPEY THE GREAT
b. 106–d. 48 B.C. Silver denarius. Head of Pompey, right. *Rev.* Galley.

3 NERO
A.D. 54–68 Copper sestertius. Head of emperor right. *Rev.* Nero with attendants distributing money to citizens.

4 JULIVS CAESAR
b. 100–d. 44 B.C. Silver denarius. Head of Caesar, right. *Rev.* Venus Victrix standing left, holding figure of victory and sceptre.

5 TIBERIVS
A.D. 14–37. Silver denarius. Head of emperor, right. *Rev.* Livia seated right PONTIF MAXIM.

6 JUDAEA
Second revolt, A.D. 132–5. Æ 25. Vine leaf and Hebrew inscription 'Second year of the deliverance of Israel'. *Rev.* Palm-tree and inscription 'Simeon'.

7 BYZANTIVM
Anonymous copper coin of the tenth or eleventh century. Bust of Christ facing.

PLATE III – EUROPEAN

1 FRANCE
Louis XIII. Silver Louis d'argent of 60 sols. 1643. By Warin.

2 FRANCE
Napoleon Bonaparte as Premier Consul. Silver five francs. Year II (23 Sept.1802–23 Sept.1803).

3 GERMANY
Bishopric of Hildesheim. Herebert von Dahlan, 1199–1215. Silver bracteate. Bishop facing left holding crozier and cross.

4 SCHLICK
Stephen and his brothers. 1487–1527. Silver taler of Joachimsthal. St Joachim standing above shield.

PLATE IV – EUROPEAN

1 ITALY
Florence. Alessandro Medici, 1533–36. Silver testone by Benvenuto Cellini. Bust, left. ALEANDER.MED.R.P. FLOREN.DVX. *Rev.* Ss Cosimo and Damian standing. S.COSMVS.S.DAMIANUS.

2 ARAGON
Alfonso V 1416–58. Gold florin. St John standing, facing. *Rev.* A lily and ARAG-O.REX.A.

3 MALTA
Grand Master Mark Anthony Zondadari, 1720–22. Silver four tari. Arms of the Grand Master, etc. *Rev.* Head of St John the Baptist on a charger.

4 SALZBURG, Archbishopric
Matthaüs Lang von Wellenburg, 1519–40. Silver half-guldener 1522.

5 SWITZERLAND Basel, city
Silver taler, undated (eighteenth century). View of the city.

Plate I.

Plate II.

Plate III.

Plate IV.

Plate V.

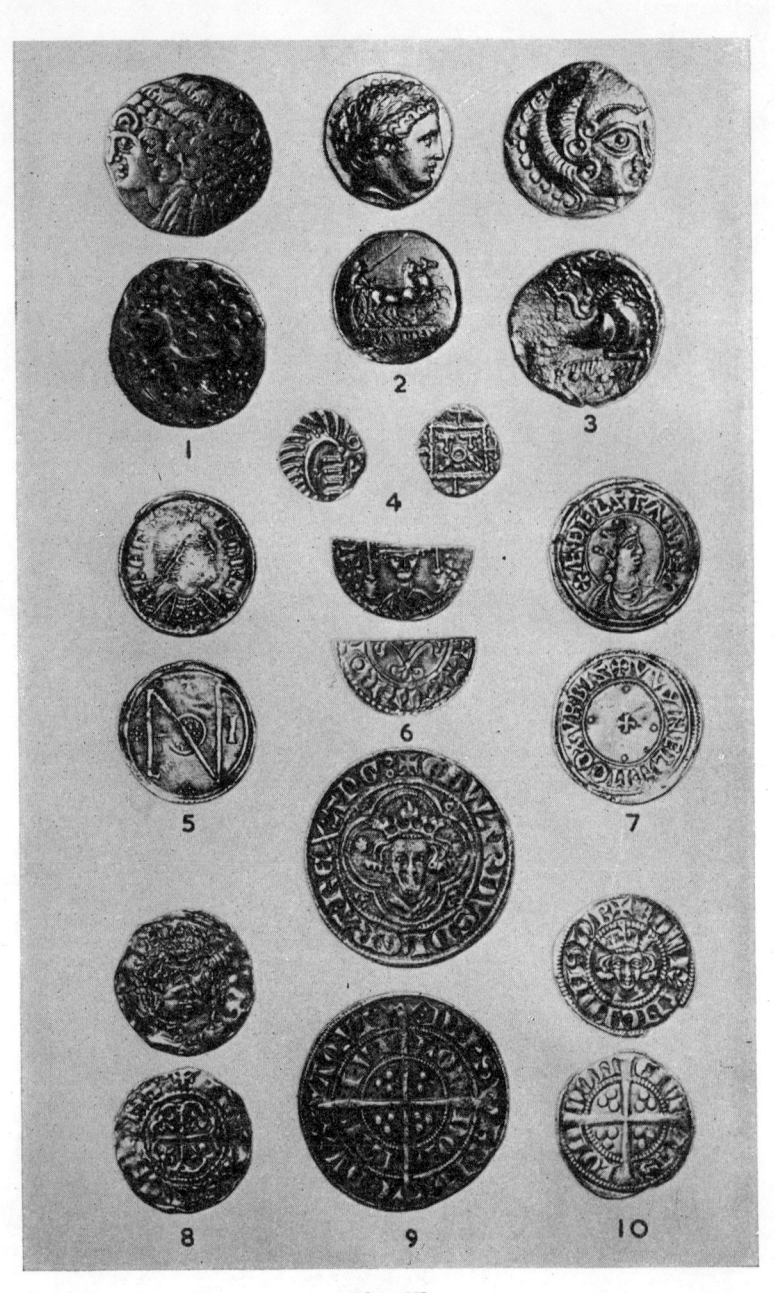

Plate VI.

Plate VII.

Plate VIII.

KEY TO PLATES

PLATE V – EUROPEAN

1 HOLLAND, kingdom
  Louis Napoleon. Silver fifty stivers. 1808.
2 SWEDEN
  Gustav Vasa. Silver riksdaler, 1543. Christ standing holding orb and hand raised in blessing.
3 RUSSIA
  Feudal princes of Ryazan. Vassili Vassilievich. Silver denga. Head in front of crescent.
4 RUSSIA
  Alexei Michailovich, silver yefimok 1655. Countermarked on a daalder of Guelders.
5 RUSSIA
  Grand dukes of Moscow. Vassili II Vassilievich the Blind, 1425–62. Silver kopeck. Duke on horseback holding lance.

PLATE VI – ENGLISH

1 ANCIENT BRITISH
  South Eastern district. Uninscribed gold stater. *c.* 100 B.C. Crude head of Apollo, left. *Rev.* Remains of crude horse.
2 GREECE, Macedon
  Philip II, 359–336 B.C. Gold stater. Head of Apollo, right. *Rev.* Chariot with driver. Prototype of coins nos. 1 and 3.
3 ANCIENT BRITISH
  Channel Islands. Billon stater. *c.* 100 B.C. Crude head, right. *Rev.* Horse galloping right; crude boar, below.
4 ANGLO SAXON
  Silver sceat *c.* sixth or seventh century A.D. Crude head, right. *Rev.* Design copied from Roman coin depicting a standard.
5 WESSEX
  Alfred, 871–99. Silver penny of London. Bust, right. *Rev.* LONDINI monogram.
6 ENGLAND
  William I, 1066–87. Silver cut halfpenny. ? Wallingford mint.
7 WESSEX
  Aethelstan, 925–39. Silver penny of Oxford. Crowned bust, right. *Rev.* VVYNELM.MO.OXVRBIS (Wynelm moneta Oxford).
8 ENGLAND
  Stephen, 1135–54. Silver penny of Shrewsbury. *Rev.* RAVENSART ON S.

9 ENGLAND
Edward I, 1272–1307. Silver groat. London mint.
10 ENGLAND
Edward I, 1272–1307. Silver penny. London mint.

PLATE VII – ENGLISH

1 EDWARD III
Post-treaty period (1369–77). Silver half-groat 'Chain mail' type. London mint.
2 HENRY VI
Annulet coinage (1422–25). Silver farthing. London mint.
3 EDWARD VI
1547–53. Silver testoon with name and portrait of Henry VIII.
4 ELIZABETH I
Silver half-crown, 1601.
5 PHILIP AND MARY
1554–58. Silver half-groat.
6 CHARLES I
Pontefract siege piece. Silver shilling, 1648. Struck in the name of Charles II after the death of Charles I.
7 CHARLES I
Pattern silver threepence by Briot, 1634.

PLATE VIII – ENGLISH

1 COMMONWEALTH
Silver crown, 1653.
2 WILLIAM III
Gold five guineas. 1701 'fine work' type.
3 CHARLES II
Gold guinea 1680. Elephant and castle below bust.
4 ANNE
Gold two guineas 1709, after union with Scotland.
5 GEORGE I
Silver shilling 1727. Roses and plumes in angles of cross on reverse.

Internal struggles for power towards the end of the ninth century split the empire principally into the separate kingdoms of France and Germany and each began to strike coins that were in some way peculiar to their own country. In France, the Capetian family succeeded to the throne and like the Carolingians before them, were content with only striking deniers and oboles, the denier being heavier than the obole by about one-third. Both deniers and oboles were struck at the Paris mint and other mints outside the royal domain also struck both types in the name of the king.

Louis IX (1226–70) struck the first gold coins for France. The gold écu was at first struck in very limited quantities; in appearance it is an attractive coin bearing the shield of France within a tressure of arcs surrounded by the legend LVDOVICVS: DEI GRACIA:FRNCOR:REX. The reverse bears the design of eight L's ending in ornate fleurs-de-lis crosswise with a rose in the centre and a fleur-de-lis in its angles. The legend is XPC.VINCIT.XPC. REGNAT.XPC.IMPERAT. Louis also struck a silver coin valued at twelve deniers and this he called the *gros tournois* after the mint of Tours where the coin was first struck. Billon coins were also issued.

Philippe le Hardi who succeeded Louis is noteworthy for introducing another type of gold coin, the gold *denier* which weighed seventy-three grains and which bore the figure of the king seated upon the throne holding the sceptre in one hand and a fleur-de-lis in the other. In the reigns that followed, other gold coins were added to the coinage; Louis X—the Angel d'or; Philippe VI—the Parisis d'or, Royal d'or, Pavillon d'or, Florin-Georges and the Chaise d'or.

The right to strike coins was, as in other countries, not only a royal prerogative; many of the French nobles, who in some cases were perhaps more powerful than the king himself, also issued coins in their own name. The counts of Anjou and Bordeaux and the dukes of Aquitaine and of Brittany are numbered among these.

During the fourteenth century the economy of France expanded considerably and as a result more mints were set up to strike coins in the king's name. By 1389 some twenty mints were in operation and to distinguish coins from one mint and another, a system of marking the dies was evolved whereby a pellet was punched under a particular letter to denote a certain mint. This system of marking is known as *points secret*. Other forms of mint marks were used at later periods, for instance, during the reign of Henry VI a lozenge, fleur-de-lis and a rose were used to indicate the mints of Arras, St Lô and Troyes respectively. It was during the reign of François I that a further system was adopted which formed the basis of the system which is still used in France today. This was the practice of placing a particular letter on the coins to indicate the mint, i.e., A—Paris, B—Rouen, C—St Lô, etc.

François II succeeded to the throne in 1559 and continued to strike testoons in the name of his father Henri II; although patterns for coins were produced depicting the facing portraits of himself and Mary Queen of Scots to whom he was married in 1558, no coins were ever struck for circulation before his death at the age of sixteen in 1560. Some of the most attractive coins in the whole French series are those struck during the reign of Louis XIII. This is partly due to the fact that three of the finest contemporary engravers were employed by the Paris mint at that time, namely Nicholas Briot, William Dupré and Jean Warin. It was the latter who was responsible for the first silver écu or Louis d'argent as it was then called, to be issued regularly in the French series (PLATE III, 1). These coins are now rare and command a high price. In the following reign—that of Louis XIV, no less than twenty-four different types of écus were struck and bear such names as *écu à la mèche longue*, *écu au buste juvenile* and *écu aux Palmes*.

The reign of Louis XVI (1774–93) may be divided into two parts, the royal coins issued prior to the enactment of the constitution in 1791 and those struck after it. The constitution separated the legislative, executive and judicial powers of France, that of the executive theoretically remaining vested in the king, whereas in fact he was virtually only a figurehead. The obverse of the coinage of this period continues to bear the portrait of the king but instead of the royal coat of arms or a similar device appearing on the reverse, the silver coins bear the figure of an angel inscribing the constitution on a tablet with the fasces (a bundle of rods with an axe in the middle) surmounted by the cap of liberty to the left and the legend REGNE DE LA LOI; below is the date in the legend L'AN 3 DE LA LIBERTE. The copper coins of this period are of various designs.

During the first three or four years of the new republic many types of coins were in use, all of them making some reference to the newly-won liberty; one of the commonest is the brass two sols bearing the head of Louis on the obverse and the fasces surmounted by the cap of liberty surrounded by a laurel wreath on the reverse.

The Directory period of 1795–9 put the coinage on a more uniform basis and in the months of April and August 1795 two directives were made establishing the decimal system for the currency, the unit of which was to be the *franc*. The highest denomination was the silver five francs which has the denomination with a wreath surrounded by REPUBLIQUE FRANCAISE, the mint letter appearing below. The reverse depicts the figure of Hercules supporting those of Liberty and Equality.

In 1802 the first coins appeared bearing Napoleon's title as Premier Consul. The highest denomination was the gold forty francs and the largest coin the silver five francs (PLATE III, 2). The legend on the coinage was changed to read NAPOLEON EMPEREUR when he assumed this title in 1804.

Following the abdication of Napoleon in 1814 the monarchy was restored and Louis XVIII remained on the throne (with the exception of the 'Hundred Days' reign of Napoleon in 1815) until his death in 1824. The royal portraits thus reappeared on the coinage until the inauguration of the Second Republic in 1848. Both the Second and the Third Republics—the latter following the second empire of Napoleon III (1852–70)—made use of the group of three figures design for the five francs originally used in the First Republic. The head of Ceres was also used as an obverse design during the Second and Third Republics. Since then, each of the succeeding republics has introduced new designs into the coinage, the Third Republic in particular introducing the design of a sower walking which has since been copied on the new 'heavy' coinage of 1960, one heavy franc being equal in value to one hundred old francs.

Germany

In common with other European countries during the tenth and eleventh centuries the coins struck in Germany were mainly of one denomination, the *denar* or *pfennig* as it later came to be called. By the twelfth century the denar had degenerated from the silver penny-sized coin to a somewhat smaller piece that was of wafer-like thinness bearing a design only on one side. These coins, known as bracteates (from the Latin *bractea*—metal foil) were struck from dies in the usual way, although possibly the dies may have been wooden, and because of the extreme thinness of the coin, the design appears raised on one side and incuse on the other. Many of these bracteates bear only a head, castle or animal design on them, but others are much larger, sometimes up to nearly an inch and a half in diameter and bear the most artistic designs together with legends that enable them to be identified exactly; the bracteate illustrated on PLATE III, 3, is from the bishopric of Hildesheim.

During the thirteenth century, European trade with the Middle Eastern countries began to increase and by the middle of the fourteenth century the whole of western Europe was using a bi-metallic currency of gold and silver. Coins of a larger denomination than the pfennig, such as the *groschen* (generally accepted at twelve pfennigs) and the *gold-gulden* made their appearance.

The division of Germany into the various principalities, each with its own ruler who issued coins and owed only nominal allegiance to the Emperors provides us with a most interesting and complex series; individual free cities and ecclesiastical authorities also issued their own coins.

Towards the latter part of the fifteenth century substantial silver deposits were discovered in Germany and this, together with the effects of the Italian Renaissance and the general shortage of gold led to the introduction in 1484 of a crown-sized coin. Originally called the *guldiner* (or, in the Tyrol, guldengroschen) these coins were subsequently called *thalers*, the name generally accepted as being derived from the word Joachimsthal, the mines from which large deposits of silver were obtained principally for the counts of Schlick, and Louis, the last independent king of Bohemia (see PLATE III, 4).

By the beginning of the sixteenth century practically every principality and free city was issuing talers, either in the name of its own ruler or in the emperor's name, one of the most prolific of these being the dukedom of Saxony. Formed from the Saxon tribes who occupied the north-west portion of Germany during the reign of Charlemagne, the area became a dukedom in 961 under Herman Billung, founder of the Billung dynasty. In

1485 Ernst and Albrecht, joint rulers of Saxony, having inherited Thuringia from their uncle Wilhelm III, divided the dukedom between them, thus forming the Ernestine Line of which Ernst became the first elector and the Albertine Line under Albrecht. Subsequent additions and alterations to the areas ruled by the Dukes of Saxony produced other principalities, each with their own coinage, i.e., Saxe-Altenburg, Saxe-Weimar, Saxe-Weimar-Eisenach, Saxe-Gotha, Saxe-Hildburghausen, Saxe-Meiningen, Saxe-Coburg-Saalfeld and Saxe-Coburg-Gotha.

By the peace of Posen in 1806 Saxony was created a kingdom, the duke Friedrich August III becoming Friedrich August I, king of Saxony. The following year he was elected duke of Warsaw re-establishing the relationship between Saxony and Poland which had been originated in the seventeenth century by Friedrich August I, duke of Saxony, who was also created king of Poland in 1697.

Many of the coins of Saxony, particularly during the eighteenth century, have fine examples of portraiture and these, together with a variety of square and even hexagonal coins struck to commemorate shooting festivals, form an attractive series.

Prussia, too, provides us with a lengthy series of coins, perhaps not so attractive as those of Saxony, but nevertheless equally important. Originally a duchy formed from the Mark of Brandenburg, it became a kingdom in 1701, the title having been granted to the Elector Friedrich III (1688–1713) in recognition of his support of Austria in the Wars of the Spanish Succession. Further additions to the territory were acquired by Friedrich the Great (1740–86) when he obtained Silesia from Maria Theresia after the War of the Austrian Succession.

The coins, almost without exception, bear the bust of the elector (or king) on the obverse with his titles around. The Prussian eagle holding the orb and sceptre sometimes appears on the reverse, although there is often a coat of arms or the crowned royal monogram, depending on the denomination.

During the seventeenth century much of the German coinage was debased due to the expense of paying for the Thirty Years War; measures which led to inflation were taken and some of the silver coins became only copper plated with silver. Coins produced by this method are usually referred to as 'Kipper and Wipper' and were struck between 1618 and 1623.

The Leipzig Convention of 1690 provided that henceforth the taler should be reduced in fineness from 27·4 grammes of pure silver to 19·35 grammes and that twelve talers instead of eight were to equal one fine mark. This was accepted as the basis for the coinage of the empire in 1738 and the new states or 'Neu-fuerstliche' Houses which had been mainly set up by the emperor as rewards for services soon found that the new specifications made striking coins unprofitable and therefore ceased coining.

The duchy of Brunswick-Lüneburg is important both historically and numismatically from the point of view of English numismatists. Georg Ludwig, elector of Hanover, became George I of England in 1714 on the death of Queen Anne because his mother Sophia was a grand-daughter of James I and all other claimants to the throne were Roman Catholics. The Anglo-Hanoverian series of coins which commenced from this date lasted until the death of William IV in 1837. These are sometimes to be found listed in the catalogues of British colonial coins because of their being struck by a king of England. Included in this series are the rather attractive talers of George I as elector bearing the Hanoverian coat of arms surmounted by the electoral cap and his titles GEORG LUD:D:G:BR:&LUN:S.R.I.EL. on the obverse and a prancing horse, the badge of Hanover, and IN RECTO DECUS on the reverse. Another series of coins issued concurrently with the preceding were the 'St Andrew' talers so-called because the figure of St Andrew is depicted on the reverse and the 'Wild Man' talers, so named for similar reasons. In 1715 following George's succession to the throne of England, many of his coins depict his portrait facing right, surrounded by his titles both as king of England and elector of Hanover. The reverse of these coins is usually devoted to the royal coat of arms that now incorporates the Hanoverian arms, the horse and the semée of hearts.

The military activities of Friedrich the Great caused a new drain on the resources of the empire and further debasement of the coinage became necessary. In Prussia, the director of the mint, Johann Philip Graumann, formed a new standard for the coinage in which the taler was to equal 16·704 grammes of silver; and this was accepted in 1750. Many of the states, however, preferred to coin on the basis of a convention signed in 1753 between Austria and Bavaria by which convention talers or specie talers were to be coined of a lighter weight. The confusion was added to when subsequently in the nineteenth century further conventions were signed establishing new standards for the taler which only made matters worse. It was not until the Franco-Prussian war of 1870–1 that the whole system was abandoned in favour of the gold standard, the *mark* being taken as the monetary unit.

The coins minted to the new standard are in many ways similar to the talers, etc. that preceded them in that the obverse is usually devoted to the head of the ruler surrounded by his titles and the reverse either bears the Imperial eagle or the coat of arms of the state. Gold coins equalling ten and twenty marks were also struck by most states and in some instances, gold five marks as well.

At the end of the First World War Germany became a republic and in the years of inflation that followed, savings became practically worthless almost overnight. Aluminium, bronze and other base metals were issued for the coinage and aluminium coins the size of an English shilling, valued at 500 marks, were quite the accepted thing. In Westphalia, a series of bronze coins was struck valued at up to a billion marks; even higher denominations were used in note form.

When the economy was stabilized once more in 1925, an extensive series of coins was issued, commemorating various events in the history of Germany. This issue, consisting of five- and three-mark pieces, depicts such events as the centenary of the City of Bremerhaven, the thousandth anniversary of the founding of Meissen, the centenary of the death of Goethe and the world flight of the "Graf Zeppelin". The art form of these coins is typically Germanic and makes quite an attractive series.

The Nazi régime left its mark on the coinage by the addition of the swastika to the reverse design and the post-war coinage struck after 1948 is somewhat unusual in that it makes use of brass-plated steel as a coining medium for some of the smaller denominations.

CHAPTER FIVE

Europe II

Austria

In the preceding chapter we have seen how France and Germany were at one time part of the Carolingian empire and how their early history is virtually inseparable. This is also the case in the early history of Austria and Germany; the possessions of the counts of Habsburg at one time included large estates in southwest Germany and following the election of Rudolph of Habsburg as emperor of Germany in 1272 the duchies of Austria and Styria passed into the possession of his sons. From this time on the power of the Habsburg family greatly increased in Austria, until various members of the family, on being elected emperors of the Holy Roman Empire, extended their rule over most of Europe.

The coinage of the archdukes of provinces such as Austria, Bohemia and the Tyrol, together with that of the emperors of the Holy Roman Empire, provides us with an attractive series of portrait coins in gold, silver and copper. The series is of especial interest if only because of two coins which are, each in their own way, unusual; the beautiful medallic taler of 1479 bearing the portraits of Archduke Maximilian and his wife, Mary of Burgundy and the Maria Theresia taler of 1780. The former is an excellent example of Renaissance portraiture whilst the latter is remarkable because of the extent to which copies of this coin have been circulated in the Middle East. Over the years the inhabitants of countries such as Abyssinia, Saudi Arabia, the Aden protectorate and the Sultanate of Muscat and Oman have become used to handling the Maria Theresia taler in trading and being fully aware of the fineness of the silver, they came to prefer these coins to any others. So much so, in fact, that until the present time various mints throughout the world—including our own Royal Mint—have found it necessary to produce copies of the taler still bearing the date 1780.

The taler of Maximilian and Mary of Burgundy is not the only example of renaissance portraiture in the Austrian series. Although of a later date (1522), the coin of Matthäus Lang von

Wellenburg (1519-40) illustrated on PLATE IV, 4, bears an equally fine portrait.

Italy

As is to be expected, by far the greatest wealth of Renaissance portraiture is found in Italy. Coins bearing superb portraits of such people as Gian Galeazzo Sforza, duke of Milan from 1416 to 1476, and Guglielmo II, duke of Monteferrato (1494-1518) may be obtained at prices far below their value as original works of art.

Many of the self-governing city states such as Venice, Milan, Mantua and Florence produced coins over a considerable period, Venice in particular striking coins in the names of the Doges which, due to the influence of Venice as a trading centre, circulated in many parts of the world. The venetian silver *matapanes* and gold *ducats* of the thirteenth, fourteenth, fifteenth and sixteenth centuries are very reminiscent in style of Byzantine coins. On the obverse of the matapanes the doge is depicted standing with St Mark surrounded by the name of the doge; the reverse bears the figure of Christ seated upon a throne. The ducat is similar, except that here the doge is kneeling before St Mark whilst on the reverse Christ is standing surrounded by stars within an oval; many Arabic copies of these ducats are found, usually with blundered legends. During the seventeenth century crown-sized silver *talari* made their appearance with the doge and St Mark design on the obverse and the winged lion of St Mark on the reverse.

The Congress of Vienna formed a kingdom out of the states of Venice and Lombardy of which Francis I, emperor of Austria, became king. During 1848, a number of demonstrations against Austrian rule forced both Venice and Milan, the capital of Lombardy to capitulate and republics were set up for a few months. Five *lire* pieces were struck in both Milan and Venice, the former being inscribed GOVERNO PROVVISORIO DI LOMBARDIA and the latter REPUBLICA VENETIA: both types are quite common.

We have seen that the Venetian coinage found its way through trade into many countries of the world and the city state of Florence too, made its mark upon European numismatics. Early coins of the republic were in the form of silver *grossi* bearing the figure of St John the Baptist on the obverse and the badge of the city, the lily, on the reverse, together with a variety of legends. Later issues of the thirteenth century included the gold *fiorino* or florin which achieved great popularity in Europe and was subsequently copied by other countries (PLATE IV, 2) including England where, although the name remained the same, it was a much larger coin depicting Edward III seated upon the throne.

Many of the great families of the Renaissance period have left us visible proof of the power that they wielded in Italy and in particular, fifteenth-century Florence is inseparable from the name of Lorenzo de Medici (1472–92), who became governor of the republic: succeeding members of the family included Alessandro de Medici who became the first duke of Florence from 1533 until 1536. The coin of the latter illustrated on PLATE IV, 1, is ascribed to Benvenuto Cellini, the famous silversmith.

Before proceeding to later Italian coins, some mention must be made of the extensive series of papal coins that has been issued by the Holy See concurrently with the regular Italian coinage. Pope Adrian I (772–95) issued the first papal coins struck in Rome and since then the coinage has been continued with some interruptions until the present day and no collection of Italian coins would be complete without the inclusion of a few specimens.

Various emblems are to be found on the coins such as the lily, rose, dove and the pelican, each of which has some religious meaning. One of the commonest, however, is the triple crown of the pope shown together with crossed keys symbolizing the power of the pope and his authority as the successor of St Peter. This design is often shown above the papal arms and is frequently used on the crown-sized *scudi*. Whilst many denominations have been issued over the centuries, some of the most eagerly sought after are the scudi which often bear delightful religious scenes on the reverse. Innocent XI issued a specimen which depicts Christ walking on the water whilst his disciples are shown in attitudes of amazement in the fishing boat; a scudo of Innocent XII depicts the Israelites collecting manna in the desert. Many of these coins also have superb portraits of the popes on them as do also the small silver denominations and the gold coins.

During the periods between the death of one pope and the election of his successor, *Sede Vacante* (seat vacant) coins were struck at the papal mints of Rome and Bologna. Their design in these cases usually consists of the arms of the papal chamberlain with the date and SEDE VACANTE on the obverse and on the reverse the Holy dove within rays together with a legend usually asking for divine guidance in the choice of a successor.

The mint of Rome is the most prolific in the papal series, but that of Bologna also struck large numbers of papal coins over the years. These were not the only mints in operation however—some thirty-six other mints were used at various times, often only for a few months when the central mint at Rome was in danger of being overrun by enemies of the pope.

The extent of Napoleonic power in nineteenth-century Europe is very well illustrated by the coinage. At the height of his success in 1808 practically the whole of Europe, with the exception of England, was under the influence of Napoleon, either being under his direct rule, protected by him or allied to him. In 1806 Napoleon created his brother Joseph king of Naples, but later replaced him by Joachim Murat his brother-in-law; Joseph afterwards became king of Spain on the abdication of Charles IV. In both the kingdoms of Naples and Spain coins were struck bearing the head of Joseph (in Italy 1806–8, in Spain 1808–13) the portraits being unmistakably those of a member of the Napoleonic family.

Spain

The Spanish currency during this period of political unrest was, not surprisingly, in some disorder. The French rule was unpopular with the people and from 1808 they were in constant rebellion. Ferdinand VII was held prisoner by the French but crudely struck coins were being issued in his name from mints in various parts of the country whilst besieged by the French. Barcelona suffered occupation by the French from 1808 until 1814 and during that time a series of coins were struck bearing the denomination (5 pesetas) within a wreath with BARCELONA above and the date below; the reverse is devoted to the arms of the city also within a wreath. Those coins of Joseph Napoleon issued from the Madrid mint during this period are in most cases comparatively common whilst those from Seville, the only other mint operating at the time, are very much rarer.

The Netherlands

Napoleon united the various provinces of the Netherlands into the kingdom of Holland in 1806 and placed his brother Louis on the throne. The coins that were issued in the name of Louis are very similar in style to those issued in Naples and Spain and are remarkably fine examples of portraiture (PLATE V, 1). Louis remained on the throne for four years and then abdicated under pressure from Napoleon who had not always agreed with the perhaps too lenient policies of his brother; the kingdom then became annexed to France. After Napoleon's defeat at the battle of Leipzig and the revolution in the Netherlands in 1813 William, Prince of Orange, was offered the throne and was crowned two years later. William struck gold coins valued at ten and five *gulden* at the mints of Utrecht and Brussels; he also continued to strike ducats similar in design to those that had been issued during the reign of Louis. The largest silver coin to be struck was the three gulden which bore the uncrowned head of William on the obverse and the crowned shield of the Netherlands on the reverse. The *rijksdaaler*, a crown-sized silver coin, was produced for the province of Utrecht in 1814, 1815 and 1816, although only those dated 1814 seem to have been struck in any quantity for circulation.

William I exchanged his possessions in Nassau for Luxembourg before he ascended the throne but Queen Wilhelmina was prevented from inheriting the grand duchy because of the Salic law and it is interesting to note that the letters G.H.V.L. (Groothertog van Luxemburg—Grand Duke of Luxembourg) are omitted from the titles.

Belgium

In 1830 Belgium became independent and the mint of Brussels which had previously produced coins for the Netherlands now began striking coins only for the new kingdom. In some instances examples are to be found of the same coin with the legend either in French or in Flemish.

Poland

Before proceeding to the Scandinavian countries, one important central European country yet remains to be discussed— Poland. Throughout her long and eventful history Poland has suffered many setbacks. During the eighteenth century she was partitioned three times, in 1772, 1793 and 1795, when Russia, Prussia and Austria annexed parts of the country. In 1918, after the First World War, Poland was formed into a republic which lasted until 1939. In September 1939 Russia and Germany invaded the country and announced that Poland had ceased to exist; a demarcation line was established between the Russian and German armies, this fourth partition annexing another 77,000 square miles to Russia and 73,000 square miles to Germany. In 1947 a new constitution was adopted which supposedly granted freedom of choice of government to the people and with amendments to this in 1952, the Polish People's Republic was established.

In common with other European countries, the early coinage of the eleventh century took the form of silver deniers. In Poland these were issued by the archbishops and were known as *wendenpfennige*, being small coins with a central cross on either side surrounded by a legend; the issue of these coins lasted some sixty or seventy years. It was not until the fourteenth century that other denominations were struck; silver gros and half-gros made their appearance, sometimes being struck for the crownlands themselves and sometimes for free cities such as Fraustadt and Danzig or the dependent territories of Lithuania and Ruthenia. Sigismund I Stary (1506–48) was the first Polish king to place his portrait on the coins with the exception of the three known specimens of a gold ducat issued by Vladislaus Lokietek (1296–1300 and 1306–33) which were struck in 1320 at the Cracow mint. The first gold coins to be struck in any quantity were those issued by Sigismund. It is interesting to note that the Cracow mint, together with that of Thorn, was originally included in Germany and belonged to the Teutonic Order. Since then, these mints have changed hands several times and are now part of Poland once more. The introduction of these higher denominations was made necessary by the increasing wealth of the country, the greatest degree of prosperity being reached during the reign of Sigismund III (1588-1632) which fact is reflected in the vast quantities of coins produced during this period.

In 1697 Friedrich August duke of Saxony was elected king of Poland and from then on his coins struck in Saxony included his Polish titles, thus qualifying them for inclusion in a collection of Polish coins. Following the defeat of Napoleon in 1814 the duchy of Warsaw passed from the possession of the kings of Saxony to the czars of Russia and at the Congress of Vienna in 1815 the czar, Alexander I (1801–25) was created king of Poland.

During the hundred and two years that Poland remained under Russian rule, various types of Russian coins were in use as well as coins valued in Polish currency. A rather peculiar situation arose during the reign of Nicholas I with regard to this in that on some of the coins the denomination is given both in Russian and Polish currency, hence we find 3 roubles=20 zlote; 1½ roubles=10 zlote; ¾ rouble=5 zlote; 30 kopecks=2 zlote and 25 kopecks=50 groze, etc. These coins were struck at both the St Petersburg and Warsaw mints.

The coinage issued during the period 1918–39 under the republic contains several commemorative coins including five-zlote pieces struck to commemorate the tenth anniversary of the creation of the republic and the revolution against the Russians in 1830.

Scandinavia

The early coinage of the Scandinavian countries is not entirely without interest to the collector of English coins since some of the kings of ninth century Britain were also kings of Denmark; due to the enormous sums of money paid to the Danes in order to buy off their raids (Danegeld) large numbers of English coins have been found in Scandinavia in general and in Denmark in particular.

The early history of the kingdoms of Norway, Sweden and Denmark is closely interwoven and for a period of some fifty odd years in the fourteenth and fifteenth centuries they were ruled as one kingdom. Sweden separated from Denmark and Norway in 1523, Gustav Vasa (1523–60) then being crowned king.

Norway was for a considerable time annexed to Denmark and remained so until 1814 when she was transferred to Sweden; it was not until 1906 that she finally gained her independence.

The early coinage of the Scandinavian kingdoms consisted of the now familiar silver penny, those struck in Denmark being similar to those being struck contemporaneously at the mints in England. Small bracteate type coins made their appearance during the eleventh to fourteenth centuries, later giving way to the silver *penning* and its multiples, struck mainly at the mints of Lund and Noestved. In Norway, Bergen was the principal mint during the thirteenth and fourteenth centuries, whilst that of Stockholm became prominent in Sweden during the fourteenth and fifteenth.

During the latter period in Sweden the coinage was one of silver *örtugo*. These were in some ways similar to the English silver pennies of Edward I in that from the latter part of the fifteenth century most examples have the head of the king facing wearing a bifoliate crown within a beaded circle and surrounded by his name; for instance SCS:ERICUS:RED and continuing on the reverse MON/ETA/STO/CHO within the arms of a cross on which is a shield bearing the three crowns of the kingdom. The coin so described was struck during the governorship of Sten Sture the elder (1471–97 and 1501–03), the type having been copied from a somewhat similar one used by Eric of Pomerania (1396–1439).

On the separation of Sweden from the Union of Kalmar in 1523 Gustav Vasa was acknowledged as king and a more comprehensive coinage was undertaken. This consisted of the one, half, and quarter *gyllen*, one *öre*, one *örtug* ($\frac{1}{2}$ öre), one *fyrk* ($\frac{1}{2}$ örtug), eighteen *penningar* and the one *penning*. A somewhat later addition was a crown-sized coin, the riksdaler, first minted in 1534 and now a very rare coin (PLATE V, 2). Gold ducats were first struck in 1568 by Eric XIV (1560–68) and his successor Johan III (1568–92) continued to strike gold coins but of different denominations: the gold gyllen and the forty-eight-mark piece together with its fractions, down to a three-mark.

In the eighteenth century we find some extraordinary copper coins struck in Sweden. Rectangular plates of copper with clipped corners and stamped with the crowned royal monogram and the date were struck in various denominations from the one *daler* up to the ten daler which measures over 2 ft. × 1 ft. and weighs nearly 40 lb.

These pieces were intended more as a form of bullion than coins for circulation and this was probably fortunate since the circulation of such cumbersome objects would no doubt have proved to be wellnigh impossible.

Denmark also struck a small number of rectangular copper coins during the seventeenth and eighteenth centuries, but these were very much smaller than their Swedish counterparts and most of them were actually intended for circulation. Some of the commonest of the earlier Danish coins are those of Christian IV (1588–1648) and many of his coins, particularly the crown-sized *speciedalers*, have fine portraits on them.

Christian VII (1766–1808) is depicted on his coinage as a rather lethargic-looking person wearing a powdered wig. This king was responsible for introducing two types of coinage, one for Denmark itself and the other for the Schleswig-Holstein duchies. The *rigsdaler species* was issued and guaranteed by the National Bank and was intended for circulation in Norway but was first circulated in Denmark as an experiment. The *species daler*, intended for Schleswig-Holstein was passed current there for sixty schillings and was guaranteed by the government.

Following the annexation of Norway to Sweden in 1814, Norway was granted a separate currency. Each country therefore adopted the practice of placing her name first after the king's name, thus, during the reign of Oscar I (1844–59) on Swedish coins we find OSCAR SVERIGES NORR. GOTH. OCH VEND. KONUNG and on Norwegian coins we find OSCAR NORGES SVER.G.OG V. KONGE (Oscar, King of Norway, Sweden, Gothland and Vendalia). This practice continued until she gained her independence in 1906.

For those collectors who specialize in commemorative coins, the Scandinavian countries provide a little material. Charles XIV Johan issued a riksdaler in 1821 to commemorate the tercentenary of the establishment of political and religious freedom; the reverse of this coin bears three medallions with the portraits of Gustav Vasa, Gustavus Adolphus and Frederik I. Gustav V issued a five-kroner in 1935 commemorating the fifth centenary of the founding of the Swedish parliament and apart from these and a number of Danish five- and two-kroner pieces such as the one commemorating the eighteenth birthday of Princess Margrethe in 1958 and the silver wedding of King Frederik and Queen Ingrid in 1960, there are few other commemorative coins.

Russia

The Russian series offers us rather more commemorative coins —eleven of them—and again as in so many other European countries the influence of Napoleon is felt, for here we find a rouble struck in 1912 that commemorates the retreat from Moscow. The reverse legend reads 1812, THIS GLORIOUS YEAR WENT BY, BUT THE HEROIC DEEDS DONE THEN WILL NEVER PASS, 1912. Other commemorative roubles include one struck in 1839 in memory of Czar Alexander I and the most recent and commonest of them all, the tercentenary of the founding of the Romanoff family 1613–1913.

Until Peter the Great (1689–1725) reformed the coinage by issuing gold, silver and copper coins after the manner of European rulers, the principal form of currency had been small silver *kopecks* and *dengi* (half kopecks) of a somewhat irregular shape. This was due to their having been struck from lengths of silver wire and for this reason they are sometimes known by the generic name of wire dengi.

The feudal princes and independent free cities such as Novgorod and Pskov also struck somewhat similar coins until the fifteenth century when Moscow under the Grand Princes absorbed most of these states, thus forming a single territory. Illustrations of two examples of the feudal coinage are to be found on PLATE V, 3, 5. In appearance the coinage suffered little change until Peter the Great, both the kopecks and dengi depict a horseman riding to the right; on the kopeck he is thrusting downwards with a lance like St George slaying the dragon, whilst on the dengi he is brandishing a sword. Some of the coins have two or more letters beneath the horse identifying the mint of issue. The reverse is devoted to an inscription in four or more lines naming the czar together with his titles, thus: CZAR AND/ GRAND PRINCE/MIKHYAL/FEDOROVICH/OF ALL RUSSIA.

Gold coins had been struck from the reign of Ivan the Terrible (1533–84) but these were not in general circulation and usually, when higher denominations than would be obtained by the use of dengi were required, silver bars or foreign coins such as Venetian ducats and German talers were used. Alexei Michailovich sought to ease the situation in 1654 by issuing crown-sized silver roubles, but discontinued doing so after a short time when he began countermarking German talers and crowns of the Netherlands instead (PLATE V, 4). It was left to Peter the Great to introduce the *rouble* for general circulation and this, together with its fractions in both silver and copper, as well as the two roubles in gold, formed the basis for the new currency. The highest denomination issued by Peter was the gold twelve-ducats which, together with most of its fractions, is remarkable for being dated with the day, month and year of issue. The issue was a very limited one and these coins only occur dated February 1st or March 1st, 1702. The four, two and one ducats are, however, not dated in this manner. It is interesting to note also that this is not the only system of dating used in the Russian series. Some of the denominations issued by Peter are dated in Kyrillic, whilst others are in Arabic and certain of the dengi are dated from the year of the Creation according to the Russian Orthodox beliefs, i.e., 7043—A.D. 1535.

The Russian series is also unusual in that between 1828 and 1845 twelve, six and three rouble pieces were struck in platinum. The metal was mined in the Ural mountains and as the sources were comparatively rich and platinum of less value than gold, it was decided to turn it into coin. They proved to be unpopular and the issue was short-lived, this contributing towards the value of these pieces which today fetch high prices.

On the foundation of the U.S.S.R., a new currency was evolved, again based on the rouble of one hundred kopecks. The central motif on nearly all the coins is the hammer and sickle on a globe within a wreath, with the exception of the early issues of 1921–30, when some of them depict a blacksmith, two workers looking towards the rising sun or a five-pointed star within a wreath.

CHAPTER SIX

England I

Early Britain

It is generally supposed that coins were not used in Britain before about the first century B.C. As in earlier civilizations before the invention of coins, the medium of exchange before this period would have been barter and since the inhabitants of these islands were primarily an agricultural people living in small closely knit communities, the medium would certainly have included cattle. During the first century B.C., however, the need was felt for a more convenient medium of exchange and consequently copies were made of those coins that had found their way to these islands in the course of trade. They consisted principally of Gaulish coins, these having been struck in central Gaul around the Saone Valley. The British copies were very crudely made of tin, having been cast in moulds, usually retaining part of the 'git' which joined one mould to another; these are considered to be the earliest of the British coins and bear a very crude representation of a head facing left on the obverse and a bull butting right on the reverse.

At the same period or perhaps a little later, other Gaulish coins of the Bellovaci tribe circulated over roughly the same south-eastern district to which the tin coins have been attributed. The Bellovacian coins are of a much higher standard of workmanship than their British counterparts and although the design is extremely crude, it can be traced to its prototype in the gold stater of Philip of Macedon bearing the head of Apollo on one side and a two-horse chariot on the other (PLATE VI, 2).

The two Belgic invasions of Britain—the first can be placed at about 75 B.C., mainly on evidence provided by Caesar—are important landmarks in British history. New coin types appeared some partly inscribed, by the Regni, Atrebates, Catuvellauni and Cantii and many of these types are again barbarous copies of the Philip stater. It is interesting to note that there are inscribed *staters* struck by Cunobolin, king of the Catuvellauni, who is the Cymbeline of Shakespeare's play. The Belgic tribes settled in an area roughly extending from Hampshire and Surrey in the south-west, to Kent in the east and along the Berkshire downs in the north. Outside this area tribes native to Britain, the Iceni, Dobuni, Brigantes, Durotriges and Trinovantes also struck their own coins somewhat in imitation of the Belgic types.

With the Claudian invasion in A.D. 43, the native coinage was demonetized and the Roman coins took their place. Although all the emperors since Julius Caesar had counted Britain as one of their possessions, it was naturally not until the Claudian invasion that any reference to British victories was made on the coinage and it was in fact not until the usurper Carausius became emperor in A.D. 287 that mints were established in Britain at London and Colchester. Coins in gold, silver and copper were struck at the London mint, the commonest being the antoninianus. Carausius also struck what are known as 'Legionary' coins; coins struck in honour of various legions which were stationed in Britain and Gaul. The reverse of these coins makes reference to a particular legion e.g. LEG IIII FLAVIA with two lions facing each other. This type is in honour of the IV (Flavia) legion whose badge was a lion or a centaur.

The supply of Roman coins for circulation in Britain was at first far from adequate and this resulted in local copies of the official coinage being produced; the commonest of these is the copy of the dupondius of Claudius. In the second century A.D. the supply of official coinage became adequate so that the imitations were not necessary.

Carausius was murdered by his financial minister Allectus who then assumed power. Allectus's reign was short (A.D. 293-6) and was comparatively uninteresting numismatically speaking except for the introduction of a new denomination, the bronze quinarius or half antoninianus, it being easily distinguished by the letter Q before the mintmark on the reverse.

Constantius Chlorus defeated Allectus in battle somewhere in Hampshire, the latter being killed in the mêlée that followed and by his death the Roman province of Britain was restored to the government of Rome. Constantius had found the island defences in a state of decay and an ever-increasing number of piratical raids by the Franks and Saxons would have to be dealt with drastically. It is not surprising, therefore, that the arrival and subsequent victory of Constantius were received by the population with some enthusiasm. Presumably because of this, or perhaps for other political reasons, a very handsome gold medallion was struck at the mint of Trier. It depicts an equestrian figure of the emperor arriving at the gates of London personified by a female figure kneeling and with the legend REDDITOR LVCIS AETERNA suggesting that Britain had been restored to the eternal light of Roman civilization.

The coins of Constantius are quite common and have been found in large numbers in this country. The follis, a bronze coin with a silver wash on it, introduced by Diocletian (A.D. 284–304), continued to be issued by Constantius and from this time on it remained the only coin that was struck at the London mint. On the death of Constantine the Great in 337 no further coins were struck in London and for the remaining years of Roman rule coins were imported from Gaul.

In 410 the Romano-British population, feeling that Constantine II was neglecting their interests—he was in fact busily engaged in defending the Rhine frontier against the Goths—revolted and expelled his governors. The coinage of Britain from this period consists entirely of 'barbarous radiates' so called because of their being crude copies of the antoninianus on which the emperor wears a radiate crown. These coins reached the lowest point of degradation at the end of Roman rule when the average size was $2\frac{1}{2}$ mm. diameter.

At the beginning of the fifth century the remaining Roman legions withdrew from Britain and darkness descended upon the island. Presumably some vestiges of Roman civilization remained, but it is not until the sixth century that any definite information exists as to the state of the country. By this time Angles, Saxons and Jutes had begun to settle in this country and a native coinage emerged. Initially these coins were copies of Merovingian types, some of which had found their way to this country through commerce, as is evident from examples found in southern England. The Merovingian kings had struck gold *tremisses* and small silver coins known as *sceats*, their design being evolved from Roman coins, and the first coins struck in Britain were gold coins of a type similar to that of the tremisses. This issue of gold was, however, shortlived and subsequently a silver sceat coinage (PLATE VI, 4), took its place in the middle of the seventh century. In many cases the types bear a distinct Merovingian flavour, whilst the later issues show the beginnings of Anglo-Saxon art. Others again show their derivation from Roman art forms as is apparent from one type in particular which is a copy of a Roman coin bearing the figures of two captives before a standard. Some of the coins are inscribed LVNDONIA and bear an attempt at portraiture on the obverse; these are rare, however, and the vast majority of Anglo-Saxon sceats at this period do not have legends on them.

The sceat coinage lasted until the end of the eighth century when it was superseded by a new coin; the *penny*. Aethelberht II of Kent (748–62) is credited with introducing the penny into the British monetary system; only two examples of these coins are known and it is apparent that the reverse design of the wolf and twins is copied from a Roman original. By this time a mint had been established at Canterbury which produced coins for the kings of Kent and the archbishops of Canterbury who had been granted the right to strike coins by their Mercian overlords. Those coins of Archbishop Aethelheard (793–805) for example, have the name of Offa on them: *obverse* AEDILHARD PONT, *reverse*, OFFA REX MERC. During the eighth century Mercia became the most powerful of the Anglo-Saxon kingdoms and following the subjugation of the kingdom of Kent at the battle of Otford in 774, Offa copied the penny and so began the first of a series of coins which was to last for the next hundred years until 874 when Burgred was deposed and Mercia became no more than a vassal state of the Viking invaders. During this hundred years, however, some of the most delightful coins in the whole Anglo-Saxon series were issued. The art form is truly Saxon and there are many pleasing portraits. One of the most interesting of them is the rare penny of Offa with the name and portrait of his wife Cynethryth; this is the only example of a Saxon lady appearing on a coin.

The kingdom of East Anglia is rather an unknown quantity. Probably it was a mere vassal state of Mercia and apart from some silver sceats of Beonna which should, perhaps, be more accurately assigned to the kingdom of Northumbria, no coins are known of East Anglia until Aethelstan I (825–840). By this time Mercian power was on the decline and the kings of East Anglia continued to strike coins until this kingdom too was absorbed into the Danelaw at the end of the ninth century. In 870 Edmund, the last

Anglican king, was murdered by the Danes for refusing to renounce Christianity and after his death those Danish settlers who had adopted his religion struck a 'memorial' coinage; large quantities of these coins must have been produced as they are quite common today.

Halfdene, the earliest of the Viking invaders of whom coins are known, occupied London in 872 and from the mint he set up there issued both pennies and, for the first time in the English coinage, halfpennies. The coins of Halfdene are extremely rare. The whole of his coinage was from the London mint and may be assigned to the period 872–5 since he transferred his capital to York in 875. Two years later Halfdene was expelled from Northumbria and was succeeded by Guthrum who later assumed the name Aethelstan when he was baptized into the Christian faith. Some rare pennies are known of Aethelstan and were probably struck after the Peace of Wedmore in 878 by which treaty after an exhausting struggle with Alfred of Wessex (871–99), he was recognized as king of East Anglia.

The coinage of the Viking invaders presents a variety of Danish symbols such as the Danish standard on coins of Sihtric (921–6), a hammer—Regnald (942–4) and a sword on coins of Eric (952–4) son of Harald Blue-tooth. The fortunes of England after the peace of Wedmore became centred in Wessex and on King Alfred. Coins had, however, been struck by the kings of Wessex as early as Beorhtric (786–802) but again these early coins are rare and it is not until the reign of Aethelwulf (839–58) who was responsible for a wider variety of types, that they become somewhat commoner. On the accession of Alfred, Canterbury was the only mint in operation, but as the power of Wessex increased and that of Mercia diminished, mints were opened at London, Gloucester, Winchester, Oxford and Exeter. Of these new mints the coins from London are perhaps the commonest; the mint of Canterbury, however, still remained very prolific. Some of Alfred's coins have portraits on the obverse and the moneyer's name on the reverse. The moneyer, the person responsible for striking the coins, placed his name on them in order that in the event of any deficiency in the standard of weight the offender could be detected at once.

The commonest coins have only a central cross on the obverse surrounded by the king's name, thus:—AELFRED REX and the moneyer's name in two lines on the reverse. A departure from the normal by Alfred was the title REX ANGLOR (King of England); and it is the first time this title was used by a king. The coin illustrated on PLATE VI, 5, is a penny from the London mint, bearing the bust of Alfred on the obverse and the monogram LONDONI on the reverse.

It was during the reign of Edward the Elder (899–925), who succeeded Alfred, that the highest peak of artistic achievement was reached. The portraiture on the coins became more delicate and there is a rare type of penny that has a building on the reverse. Some coins have the Hand of Providence on them, whilst others again depict a bird holding a twig. One delightful coin has a drawing of a church which probably refers to the Minster at Winchester which was completed in Edward's reign.

Aethelstan (925–39) continued the fight against the Danes and the title AETHELSTAN REX TOTIVS BRITANNIAE is to be found on some of his later coins. It was Aethelstan who decreed at a Witanagemot at Grately in 928, that every burgh or town should have a mint with from one to eight moneyers depending on its importance, thus providing that a single coinage should be current throughout the country, and that the dies were to be engraved in London. Thus eight moneyers were appointed to London, seven to Canterbury, six to Winchester, etc. At Grately, too, it was decreed that the penalty for forgery should be the loss of a hand which was then to be nailed up in the smithy or, if the accused desired to clear himself of the charge, the hand that struck the coin should be submitted to 'the ordeal of the hot iron'.

It is to Edgar (959–75) that the credit for finally conquering the Danes must go and by this he became the first real king of all England. Thirty-one mints were in operation during Edgar's reign, producing well-made pennies and from one particular mint, round halfpennies. These latter coins had occasionally been struck in the past by other kings but sometimes pennies cut in half were used as a more convenient method of producing a smaller denomination. Although Edgar had conquered the Danelaw, the country was now troubled by the Danish raiders who were plundering the coasts and during the reign of Aethelred II (979–1016) these raids became ever more frequent. Eventually the position became so desperate that Aethelred was forced to buy off the raiders by payment of 'Danegeld'. In all, payment was made to a total of 155,000 lb. of silver, a very large part or perhaps all of it in coin: many large hoards of Aethelred's coins having been found in Scandinavia testify to this fact.

Upwards of sixty mints were in operation during Aethelred's reign. All of the coins bear his portrait and for the first time the king is shown holding the sceptre. Many of the coins bear a long cross on the reverse, thus facilitating their division into smaller denominations.

On St Brice's day (13 November) Aethelred arranged for the massacre of all the remaining Danes in England for fear of assassination. In retaliation for this Swein, king of Denmark, invaded England in 1003, penetrating farther inland than any earlier raiding party. In succeeding years Swein returned with armies led by his two sons Harald and Cnut, the latter eventually becoming king of England on the death of Aethelred.

Harald died in 1019 and Cnut by his brother's death became both king of Denmark and England and married into the Saxon dynasty by marrying Emma, the widow of Aethelred II. The coins of Cnut are notable for the introduction of the crown on the king's head.

Harthacnut, Cnut's only legitimate son, succeeded to the kingdoms of England and Denmark in 1035 on the death of his father but his half-brother Harald, who was in England at the time, seized power and reigned until 1040 when Harthacnut succeeded in establishing himself on the throne of England.

The coins of Harald I (1035–40) consist of only two types, the first being similar to the last type of Cnut, i.e., the reverse design consisting of a central cross formed of four jewels surrounded by the moneyer's name and mint. Harthacnut also issued only two types, the first again being similar to that of Cnut's last type.

In 1042 Harthacnut died whilst drinking at the wedding feast of one of his father's retainers and Edward 'the Confessor', son of Aethelred II was elected king and crowned at Winchester on Easter day 1043. The coins of Edward's reign are of interest if only because of three departures from the normal Saxon coin types. The first had a seated figure of the king on the obverse, another type was struck on a smaller flan than usual, thus giving the impression that the coins are halfpennies and the third was the facing portrait of the king as against the usual profile.

On the death of Edward in 1066 Harold Godwinson, earl of

Wessex was elected king. Owing to the short duration of Harold's reign only one type of penny was issued. It bears the bust of the king on the obverse, the sceptre in front of it sometimes being omitted. Despite the fact that there is only one type of penny, the coins of Harold are fairly common due to their being upwards of forty mints in operation at the time.

CHAPTER SEVEN

England II

Normans and Plantagenets

WILLIAM I landed in England on 14 October 1066 and with his archers, crossbowmen and heavily armed infantry defeated the somewhat lighter armed English and a new era dawned in England. William reigned for twenty-one years and during that time eight types of pennies were issued. All bear the bust of the king on the obverse and as was now the common practice, all the portraits are shown wearing a crown. Six types have a full face portrait, whilst the other two are profiles, one facing left and the other right. The commonest type is the eighth or PAXS type, so called because those letters appear in the angles of the cross on the reverse. Until 1833, however, this was the rarest of the eight types, then a hoard of more than 6,000 of these pennies was discovered, thus making it the commonest. PLATE VI, 6, illustrates a cut halfpenny of William.

William II succeeded his father as king of England whilst the dukedom of Normandy went to his elder brother Robert. William II struck five types which are very similar in style to those of his father.

One of the reasons for the frequent changes in type was the fact that each time a new type was produced the moneyers paid the king's dues of twenty shillings. The dies were engraved in London by the aurifaber or goldsmith who made the moneyers a reasonably heavy charge for his work. The fact that all the dies were engraved in London produced a uniform coinage throughout the country and one in which irregularities of style (due to local manufacture) which might lend itself more easily to forgery, could be minimized. Despite the severe penalties for forgery or the production of coins of poor quality and weight, the coinage under Henry I (1100–35) had become rather poor and many coins, although struck at the official mints, were struck in base silver or of a low weight. This situation gave rise to the following entry being recorded in the *Anglo-Saxon Chronicle* for the year 1125:

'In this year sent the King Henry, before Christmas, from Normandy to England and bade that all the mint-men that were in England should be mutilated in their limbs; that was, that they should lose each of them the right hand and their testicles beneath. This was because the man that had a pound could not lay out a penny at a market. And the Bishop Roger of Salisbury sent over all England, and bade them all that they should come to Winchester at Christmas. When they came thither then were they taken one by one and deprived each of the right hand and the testicles beneath. All this was done within the twelfthnight. And that was all in perfect justice because that they had undone all the land with the great quantity of base coin that they all bought.'[1]

The Margam annals differ from the above in that they state that ninety-four of the moneyers were mutilated.

That the traders of the period were doubtful as to the quality of the coins is proved by their making small cuts in them to test the fineness. The public, however, as a general rule disliked the practice and often refused to accept coins with cuts in them; this led to all those coins that may be dated as being struck between about 1112 and 1128 being cut at the mint before being issued. It is interesting to note that those of Henry's coins issued after the latter date do not have the cut so perhaps the stern measures of 1125 had some effect and gave the populace confidence in these coins.

On the death of Henry I in 1135 England entered into a period of unrest owing to the fact that Henry had designated his daughter Matilda as his successor; a move which was unpopular with many of the Norman nobles. They in turn invited Stephen, count of Blois and grandson of William I to become king. The claims of the Empress Matilda were supported by the Angevin party and a state of civil war ensued. The Angevin party controlled the whole of the western half of the country whilst Stephen held eastern and central England and in 1138 David, king of Scotland came south to lend support to Matilda. In 1141 the Angevins captured and imprisoned Stephen for a time and Matilda was crowned at Winchester; eight years later, however, she abdicated in favour of her son Henry, duke of Anjou. After more confused fighting,

[1] *The Anglo-Saxon Chronicle*—Rev. Ingram's translation.

Stephen eventually made peace with Henry at the Treaty of Wallingford in 1153, recognizing him as his heir.

The coinage of the period 1135–53 is one of exceptional interest because of the many irregular issues and the so-called baronial issues. Of the latter, coins were struck by Eustace FitzJohn, Robert de Stuteville, Robert and William of Gloucester, Brian Fitzcount or Baldwin de Redvers, Patrick, earl of Salisbury and Henry of Blois, bishop of Winchester. Many of Stephen's coins are badly struck owing to the obverse dies being defaced. This was possibly an attempt by the moneyers to cover themselves when they were in danger of being captured by the enemy. (PLATE VI, 8.)

There were three mints that definitely produced coins for Matilda; Bristol, Oxford and Wareham, and all of her coins are copies of the first type of Stephen: crowned head facing right with the title IMPERATR or MATILDIS IMP on the obverse and a cross moline with fleurs-de-lis in the angles with the moneyer's name and mint around it.

In 1154, the year after the Treaty of Wallingford, Stephen died and Henry of Anjou, in accordance with the terms of the treaty, became king as Henry II. Until 1158 when a new type of penny was introduced, the mints continued striking coins from Stephen's dies and although the new 'Tealby' coinage, as it is known from the large hoard found at Tealby in Lincolnshire, was made the sole currency in England no attempt at improving the standards seems to have been made. These coins are usually poorly struck and the whole of the legend is very rarely, if at all, to be found on the coins. The poor state of the coinage and the inefficiency of the moneyers reached such a climax that in 1180 a French goldsmith, Philip Aimer of Tours was called to England to design a new type. The new design that was to last for the next sixty-seven years was still no great improvement from the artistic viewpoint over the Tealby coinage. The coins were, however, better struck and since they all bear the name HENRICVS REX it is a matter of some difficulty to decide which may be attributed to the reign of Henry II (1154–89), Richard I (1189–99), John (1199–1216) or to Henry III (1216–72). The facing head is a crude one, the design being punched out in the die in a series of curved lines, dots and crescents; the lettering is made up in the same manner. The central design on the reverse is a small voided cross contained within a beaded circle, thus giving rise to the generic term 'short-cross pennies'. There were no round halfpennies and farthings of this issue so again the practice of cutting the penny into its fractions was carried out, the cross on the reverse facilitating this.

The short-cross coinage lasted until 1247 when only four mints remained in operation and the practice of 'clipping' the coins, i.e. shearing off small portions for the illegal melting of the silver had become so prevalent that the cross on the reverse was extended to the edge of the coin. Those clipped pennies on which the four ends of the cross were not visible were declared illegal. The new long-cross pennies also bore for the first time the numeral after the king's name, viz., HENRICVS REX TERCIVS later abbreviated to HENRICVS REX III.

Mention must be made here of a coin of particular numismatic interest; the gold penny. In 1252 the city state of Florence issued a new gold coin called the fiorino or florin which quickly found favour in Europe owing to the fact that there had been practically no gold coinage struck in Europe since the ninth century. Henry III attempted to establish a gold currency in England also and ordered his goldsmith William to produce pennies struck in pure gold and valued at twenty silver pence. The coin is a very handsome one showing the king seated on the throne holding the orb and sceptre with the legend HENRICVS REX III. The reverse has a long voided cross with roses and pellets in the angles surrounded by WILLEM ON LVNDE. Unfortunately the coin proved to be unpopular for the issue was only very limited and it is now extremely rare. One of the seven known specimens (three of which are in the British Museum) was offered for sale in London in 1955 and realized £1,950.

For the first eight years of the reign of Edward I long-cross pennies continued to be struck with the name of Henry III. In 1279, however, the working of the mint was reorganized and placed under the control of the master-worker, later the Master of the Mint, and a new coinage was struck.

The new coins were very much better designed than the long-cross pennies and show the facing bust of the king wearing the crown with rather long wavy hair flowing from beneath it (PLATE VI, 10). The indentures of 1279 also ordered a new coin to the value of fourpence to be struck—the groat (PLATE VI, 9) the name probably being copied from the French coin of an equivalent size which was known as a gros tournois. The design for the groat was bold and imaginative, the bust of the king being shown within a quatrefoil and a beaded border and the legend EDWARDVS DI: GRA:REX ANGLIE and continuing on the reverse DNS HIBN E DVX AQVT LONDONIA CIVI (Edward Dei Gratia Rex Angliae Dominus Hiberniae et Dux Aquitaniae). The titles Dei Gratia (By the Grace of God) and Dominus Hiberniae et Dux Aquitaniae (Lord of Ireland and Duke of Aquitaine) appear on English coins for the first time.

The issue was a short-lived one and the groats are therefore quite rare, eagerly sought after by collectors and good specimens command a high price. Many of them have, however, been gilded and show signs of having been mounted at an early date. As well as the new groats, round halfpennies and farthings were also ordered by the indenture, the farthings being particularly small—they have a diameter of some 10 millimetres—and one can imagine how easy it must have been to lose them.

As the responsibility for the fineness of the coins now rested upon the master-worker it was no longer necessary to put the moneyer's name on the coins so the mint name only appeared. The exception to the rule is, however, that of the moneyer Robert de Hadleie who struck coins for the Abbot of Bury St Edmunds, who had minting rights. The Abbot of Reading also struck coins during the reign of Edward I and his coins are distinguished by an annulet below the king's bust.

Owing to the quantities of continental esterlings (coins made of base silver in imitation of the Edward I penny) circulating in this country at the time, large quantities of English pennies were being exported to the low countries for their bullion value so that in 1300 the esterlings were devalued to halfpennies and in 1301 they were called in and melted down. These imitations are sometimes known as 'crockards' and 'pollards' owing to the fact that some depict the bust wearing a chaplet of roses whilst others, if issued by an ecclesiastical mint, have the shorn or 'polled' head of a priest.

The striking of pennies of the general type of Edward I (PLATE VI, 10) continued through the reign of Edward II (1307–27) and for the first nine years of Edward III. Slight variations in style and lettering enable us to distinguish the pennies struck by Edward I from those by Edward II. The Edward III pennies are somewhat easier to distinguish owing to the use of Lombardic 'n's' instead of Roman 'N's' and pellet stops in the legend.

In 1335 the striking of halfpennies and farthings was again ordered: no pennies were called for due to the shortage of silver and it was not until 1344 that pennies reappeared. In that year it was decided to issue a gold coinage and consequently two Florentine goldsmiths were appointed joint master-workers of the mint. They produced a series of lovely coins, the largest being the florin valued at six shillings and of 23 carat $3\frac{1}{2}$ grains fine gold. The half-florin or *leopard* and the quarter-florin or *helm* were also struck and derive their names from the leopard wearing the royal crown and mantle on the former and a helmet with a crest of a royal lion standing on the cap of maintenance on the latter. The florin itself depicts the crowned full length figure of the king seated on the throne holding the orb and sceptre, the type being copied from the Parisis d'or of Philip IV of France. The florin and its fractions were only a short lived issue and in August of the same year the florin was superseded by the *noble* valued at 6s 8d and its fractions the half and quarter. The noble and half-noble depict the crowned figure of the king standing in a ship holding a shield and shouldering a sword; this design, it is said, makes reference to the English naval victory at Sluys in 1340.

Edward disputed the claim of Philippe de Valois to the French throne on the death of Charles IV as his own mother was a sister of Charles and in 1337 Edward declared war against Philippe de Valois, calling himself king of France. On those coins issued in 1344 the French title is added to the English, a practice which lasted until 1360 when, at the Treaty of Bretigny, Edward renounced his claim to the French throne. In 1369, however, the quarrel with France flared up again, war was declared once more and the French titles replaced on the coinage.

During this reign, English coins began to be struck at Calais, the mint opening in 1363. Silver, and later gold coins, were struck at this mint and may be distinguished from those struck at other mints by a variety of marks; the letter 'C' on the early gold coins, a flag on the stern of the ship, an annulet on the king's breast and other marks made the identification fairly easy.

On the accession of Richard II no attempt was made to make new dies and his earliest coins are struck from dies used in the previous reign. Later, however, when new dies were cut they remained very similar in style to Edward's coins. Only gold coins were struck at the Calais mint during Richard's reign.

In 1399 Henry, son of John of Gaunt, duke of Lancaster, forced Richard to abdicate and supported by the nobles was acclaimed king as Henry IV. Owing to the fact that the English currency was undervalued compared with continental coins, large amounts of bullion were being exported from this country with the result that fewer and fewer coins were struck during Henry's reign. The coins may be divided into two types; the heavy coinage of 1399–1412 with the noble weighing 120 grains and the light coinage 1412–13, when the weight of the noble was reduced to 108 grains. The light coinage is distinguished from the heavy by three marks which appear on the coins; the trefoil, a design like the three leaves of clover, the annulet (a circle) and a pellet. It is interesting to note that since no groats were struck of Henry's heavy coinage, when it was decided to issue them again in 1412 for the light coinage, some of Richard's dies were used with the name altered.

The coinage of Henry V who succeeded his father is comparatively common, the general type remaining the same. The use of privy marks, a variety of marks such as we have noted on the light coinage of Henry IV, probably altered every three months or so, is maintained. Dies used during the previous reign were altered to incorporate the new privy marks and were used again.

The Calais mint was not used at all during the reign of Henry V and it was not until 1424 in the reign of Henry VI that coins were again struck there, silver coins from the groat to the farthing being produced in large quantities. Gold coins were only produced for four years at the Calais mint and in London very little gold was struck after about 1433, this situation again being brought about by the export of large quantities of gold coins to the Continent.

The ecclesiastical mints of York and Durham are again in evidence during this reign and produced coins variously for Archbishops Kemp (1425–52) and William Booth (1452–64) of York and Bishops Langley (1406–37), Robert Neville (1438–57) and Laurence Booth (1457–76) of Durham.

Apart from the privy marks altered every few months, other marks, altered only every three years or so were used during the reign of Henry VI; the reign can therefore be divided into eleven periods according to these marks, thus enabling us to date coins to within a very few months of their issue.

The Wars of the Roses began in 1455 and the subsequent defeat of the Lancastrian army at Mortimer's Cross in Herefordshire by Edward, duke of York, in 1461 enabled the Yorkists to proclaim Edward king. His first reign of some nine years is, like that of Henry IV, divided into a heavy and a light coinage (1461–4 and 1464–70). The heavy coinage consists mainly of silver coins and these were only produced in small quantities, the commonest coins being the groats and the pennies produced at the Durham mint from dies made locally. The amount of gold produced was almost negligible, and the noble weighing 108 grains was the only denomination struck and today only two examples are known of this exceedingly rare coin. In 1464 the weight of the penny was reduced from 15 to 12 grains and in 1465 an indenture completely reforming the gold coinage was issued. A new coin to be called the *ryal* or *rose-noble* valued at 10*s* (as against the noble's 6*s* 8*d*) and weighing 120 grains was ordered. Half and quarter-ryals were also struck. Two other new coins were struck, the angel valued at 6*s* 8*d* (wt. 80 grs.) and the half-angel at 3*s* 4*d*. The design of the ryal is similar to that of the noble, but the cross on the centre of the reverse is replaced by a Yorkist rose superimposed on a sun in splendour. The half-ryal is similar in design to the ryal, but the quarter-ryal has the royal arms in either a quatrefoil or a tressure of eight arcs on the obverse: the reverse is similar to that of the ryal and half-ryal. The obverse of the *angel* depicts St Michael slaying the dragon with the legend EDWARD DI GRA REX ANGL Z FRANC DNS HYB whilst the reverse bears a shield with the royal arms on a ship and PER CRVCEM TVAM SALVA NOS XPC REDEMPTOR (By Thy Cross save us, O Christ our Redeemer). The half-angels have the shield and ship on the obverse and St Michael on the reverse with the legend O CRVX AVE SPES VNICA (Hail! O Cross, our only hope).

Higher prices were offered for silver by the Tower mint which resulted in larger quantities of bullion being brought to the mint instead of it being exported. The increased production led to new mints being opened in 1465 at Bristol, Coventry and Norwich and the Royal mints were reopened at Canterbury and York. Bristol remained in operation until 1472 but Coventry and Norwich closed some two months after opening.

After the return to England of Richard Neville (Warwick the Kingmaker) Henry VI was released from the Tower where he had been confined after his capture following his defeat and flight at the battle of Mortimer's Cross.

Henry was restored to the throne and remained in power from October 1470 until April 1471. Henry's coins of this period are similar to those of Edward IV, the name only being altered. As might be expected of such a short reign, none of the coins is particularly common, the rarest being the half-angel from the Bristol mint which also struck halfpence.

On Edward's return to England, Warwick was slain at the battle of Barnet fought on Easter Day 1471, and Henry was again committed to the Tower, being murdered the same night. Angels and half-angels were the only gold coins struck during Edward's second reign, but groats, half-groats, pennies and halfpennies were struck in quite large quantities especially by the ecclesiastical mints of York and Durham.

Edward IV died on 9 April 1483 and his son, Edward, Prince of Wales, then aged twelve, was placed under the guardianship of his uncle Richard, duke of Gloucester. Richard was recognized as Protector and the coronation of Edward was fixed for 22 June. Edward, together with his younger brother, were lodged in the Tower on Richard's orders where sometime between June and October they were murdered. Richard, having arranged to be offered the crown by a deputation of the nobles and citizens of London, assumed the throne himself on 25 June.

It is a matter for some conjecture which coins may be attributed to the period when Edward was under the Protectorship of Richard. There is a series of angels, half-angels, groats, pennies and halfpennies which bear the initial mark of a halved sun and rose which may or may not belong to this period. There are, however, a very few angels, groats and pennies which bear the initial mark of a boar's head, the personal badge of Richard, on the obverse which do definitely belong to these few weeks.

Richard's reign was a short and violent one and three years after his coronation he was killed at the Battle of Bosworth. The coins of Richard's reign are therefore quite rare, the commonest of them being the groat. Three mints were in use, the principal being London. Groats and pennies were struck at the royal mint of York and pennies were also struck at the York ecclesiastical mint for Archbishop Rotherham. Bishop Sherwood also issued coins from the Durham mint.

CHAPTER EIGHT

England III

Tudors and Stuarts

On the death of Richard Plantagenet on 22 August 1485, Henry Tudor, son of Edmund Tudor and Margaret, great granddaughter of John of Gaunt, acceded to the throne as Henry VII. Henry's policy was a peaceful one both internationally and internally and he set about the task of improving the state of England with vigour; and on his death in 1509 he left England in a flourishing condition with the royal coffers well filled. The coinage, which had suffered from the long period of political unrest was extensively altered; new denominations both in gold and silver were struck and for the first time in English history a real attempt at portraiture was made on the coins. In 1489 a new gold coin was ordered. It was to be worth twenty shillings and to be called a *sovereign*: the coin is a large one having a diameter of some 42 millimetres and weighing 240 grains. Having such a large flan to work on, the artist was able to depict the splendour of the Tudor period in all its glory. On the obverse the king is shown seated on the throne in his robes, wearing the royal crown and holding the orb and sceptre. The reverse design is the royal arms centred on a full blown Tudor rose. In 1494 Alexander of Brugsal was appointed engraver to the mint and a somewhat different type of sovereign was produced: although the design remained essentially the same, the new coin was rather more ornate and the figure of the king is better proportioned than on the earlier type. Alexander was also responsible for the engraving of a profile groat and portrait *testoon*, or shilling, that was issued during the last few days of Henry's reign.

London was again the principal mint and during the last fifteen years of the reign some 31,000 lb. of gold and 164,000 lb. of silver were turned into coin. The ecclesiastical mints of Canterbury, York and Durham were again in evidence.

Henry VIII was the son of his father's marriage with Elizabeth of York and he succeeded to the throne of England at the age of eighteen. He was handsome, accomplished and pleasure-loving and for the first fifteen years of his reign did nothing to alter the design or portraiture on the coinage from that used by his father. His coins can be distinguished from those of Henry VII by the numeral VIII after the king's name or by the new mint marks, crowned portcullis and castle. Despite the enormous wealth left by his father, Henry managed to squander most of it and during the last years of his reign the currency was debased to provide more revenue. Gold coins were reduced to 20 carats fine and the silver to one part silver to two parts alloy. Consequently these late silver coins are usually found in poor condition with the copper showing through on the highest parts of the design, resulting from excessive wear, thus earning Henry the nickname 'Old Coppernose'. Silver testoons bearing the facing bust of the king (PLATE VII, 3) are reminiscent of the famous paintings of the king by Holbein.

In 1526 Cardinal Wolsey was ordered to alter the standard of the coinage to that of foreign countries to prevent any further drain of English coin to the Continent resulting from foreign coins circulating in England at a disproportionately high value. Apart from altering the values of existing coins, new gold coins of a baser metal were issued. One of these was the gold 'crown of the rose' which has the royal coat of arms on the obverse and a Tudor rose on the reverse. This coin was equal to 4s 6d, and was the first of the 'crown' denomination that was continued in subsequent reigns both in gold and as a silver coin equalling 5s. Another new coin was the George-noble, smaller than the angel of previous reigns, but having the same value of 6s 8d. This is a delightful piece depicting on the obverse St George slaying the dragon and a Tudor rose mounted on a ship on the reverse; the half-George-noble also issued has a similar design. These rare coins (a single specimen of the half-George-noble is known) are particularly interesting because of the letters 'h k' standing for Henry and Katherine of Aragon which appear either side of the mast on the reverse.

Large numbers of coins were again issued by the ecclesiastical mints of York, Durham and Canterbury. Cardinal Wolsey, being both archbishop of York and bishop of Durham from 1523 struck coins with his initials TW on them at both of these mints. Other coins of York consist of those issued by Archbishop Bainbridge with the initials XB on them and also of Archbishop

Edmund Lee (LE or EL). The mint of Durham struck coins for Bishops Rothall and Tunstall as well as for Wolsey. Canterbury struck coins for Archbishops Warham and Cranmer.

In 1546 a mint was opened at Bristol to supplement the work at the Tower mint; other mints were also opened at Southwark, together with royal mints at York and Canterbury.

In 1548 a mint was opened at the former palace of the bishops of Durham at Durham House in the Strand and although Henry had died in the previous year, his son Edward continued striking coins with his father's portrait and titles for the first few months of his reign (PLATE VII, 3). Durham House struck a peculiar groat during this period bearing the bust of Henry three-quarters-facing wearing the crown at rather a rakish angle and the reverse legend REDDE CVIQVE QVOD SVVM EST (Render unto each that which is his). Continuing the precedent of his grandfather, Edward continued to strike shillings with his portrait in profile, but of two different standards of fineness. In 1549 a small shilling weighing 60 grains was produced from 8 oz. fine silver and a somewhat larger one, weighing 80 grains from 6 oz. silver. In 1551 the standard of silver was restored to 11 oz. fine and the base shillings were superseded by a larger coin with a full face portrait. It was, however, found to be impossible to call in all of the base shillings and many continued to circulate together with the fine issue until the early years of Elizabeth's reign. The year 1551 also saw the first issue of the new crown pieces struck in silver. The king is depicted on a galloping horse richly caparisoned with the date below.

The gold coins of Edward's reign are delightful but unfortunately rare; two of the half-sovereigns issued between January 1548 and April 1550 have charming portraits of the young king who was aged eleven at the time, and show a remarkable feeling for portraiture.

Edward was a delicate youth, much inclined to study and was strongly influenced in his decisions by the duke of Northumberland, allowing himself to be persuaded to alter the terms of Henry VIII's will, thereby excluding Henry's daughters Mary and Elizabeth from the succession in favour of Lady Jane Grey, Northumberland's daughter-in-law. It has been suggested that Northumberland, on Edward's falling ill, helped a little by giving him a small dose of poison; there is, however, no evidence of

ENGLAND III 85

this. At any rate Edward died on 21 June 1553 and Northumberland informed Jane Grey that she was queen, a prospect that she did not entirely relish. Her reign lasted only eleven days and consequently no coins are known of her.

Jane was succeeded by Mary whose coins can be divided into two periods, those issued in her name alone before her marriage to Philip II of Spain and those issued after the marriage, which include his name. Seven denominations were issued in her own name, four gold and three silver. The angel is the commonest of these gold coins and it is very often found pierced for use as a 'touch piece'. Touch pieces were hung around the neck of the sick by the king at the ceremony of 'touching for the King's Evil'; the coin, having been touched by the king, was supposed to heal the patient. This practice was discontinued by Queen Anne.

The silver coins of this first period of Mary's reign, consisting of groats, half-groats and pennies, were unfortunately struck in low relief so that the portrait quickly becomes very worn; the commonest of these coins is the groat.

In January 1554 Mary was married by proxy to Philip II of Spain, the religious ceremony taking place in the following July. Thereafter her coins also include Philip's name on them (PLATE VII, 5). Angels and half-angels were the only gold coins issued, but the silver shilling and sixpence reappear and bear the portraits of both Philip and Mary face to face, after the manner of Spanish coins.

On the accession of Elizabeth in 1558, the financial resources of England were in a sorry state, and they continued to be drained away as a result of the country helping to pay for the war in which she was allied with Spain against France. Those shillings of Edward VI that were still in circulation were now re-valued as the public refused to accept them at the full rate: the basest were valued at $2\frac{1}{4}d$ and were countermarked with a greyhound's head whilst those with a higher silver content were valued at $4\frac{1}{2}d$ and countermarked with a portcullis. Elizabeth's coins are of an almost bewildering variety; there are many variations in the legends and the types of busts and more denominations were issued than ever before. The 'fine' sovereign of 30s first issued by Mary was again issued and in 1545 the *pound sovereign* of 20s was also struck, together with its half. The silver crown and half-crown (PLATE VII, 4) were again issued and for the first time threepences, threehalfpence, and three-farthings were struck. The latter, despite its small size, still manages to boast a portrait of Elizabeth on the obverse. To facilitate easy identification of the various small denominations a rose was placed behind the Queen's head on the obverse and the date above the shield on the reverse on alternate denominations from the shilling downwards, thus we find: *shilling*, no rose or date, *sixpence*, rose and date; *groat*, no rose or date; *threepence*, rose and date; *half-groat*, no rose or date; *threehalfpence*, rose and date; *penny*, no rose or date; *three-farthings*, rose and date; *halfpenny*, obverse portcullis, reverse cross with pellets in angles.

In 1560 an important development in coin production took place. Eloye Mestrelle, an employee of the Paris mint left in disgrace and was given employment at the Royal mint at the Tower. He was paid £25 per annum and free accommodation in the upper part of the mint, and between 1561 and 1571 he struck both gold and silver coins with his new presses which were powered by horses. Despite the fact that these coins are very much better struck than the old hammered issues, they were discontinued after 1571 as the workers, fearing for their jobs, raised objections to the new machinery and for one reason or another Mestrelle fell from favour and the former coining methods were restored in 1572. Mestrelle, incidentally, was hanged in 1578 for counterfeiting. The coins that were struck during this ten-year period consist of the gold *half-sovereign*, *crown* and *half-crown* and the silver shilling, sixpence, groat, threepence, half-groat and three-farthings.

The fact that not enough small change was available had long been the cause of much grievance amongst the poorer people of the country and many local tradesmen had tried to alleviate the difficulty somewhat by issuing their own lead tokens. These could be redeemed for coin of the realm by their customers whenever they wished and consequently most people were glad to accept them. The government had already made several abortive attempts to suppress them but it was not until 1613 when James I granted a licence to Lord Harrington to manufacture copper farthings (the profits being shared between them) that the issue of traders' tokens was stopped. In 1615 after the death of Harrington his widow sold the patent to the Duke of Lennox who continued to strike coins of this denomination. Subsequently *his* widow, the

Duchess of Richmond, also struck them; later the patent was purchased by Lord Maltravers.

When James ascended the English throne in 1603 he had already been king of Scotland for thirty-six years. He had succeeded to the Scottish throne at the somewhat unreasonably early age of one on his mother's forced abdication. His claim to the English throne was through his great-grandmother, Margaret, daughter to Henry VII and wife of James IV of Scotland.

The union of England and Scotland under one monarch is recorded on the coins by the addition of the Scottish titles after the English and the arms of Scotland being added to the shield on the reverse. Some of the coins have a definite Anglo-Scottish flavour as witness the thistle-crown, a gold coin with a crowned rose on the obverse and a crowned thistle on the reverse and the silver half-groat, penny and halfpenny which also bear these emblems.

The silver crown and half-crown revert to the original design instituted by Edward VI and depict the king on horseback. Shillings and sixpences bearing the customary crowned bust of the king were also struck. The Scottish coins at this time were at a ratio of twelve to one, so that the Scottish sixty-shilling piece was current for five shillings English, the thirty shillings was current for 2s 6d and the half shilling equalled the English halfpenny, etc. These coins are the same size as their English equivalents and are similar in design, but they can be identified as being either English or Scottish by the thistle which appears on the trappings of the horse on the Scottish sixty shillings and thirty shillings and the rose on the English crown and half-crown. The smaller denominations may be identified by the crown on the king's bust. The Scottish crown has three fleurs-de-lis with two crosses between them whilst the English crown has three crosses and two fleurs-de-lis. On later Scottish coins of James there is a Scottish lion in the first and fourth quarters of the arms on the reverse.

Charles I succeeded his father James in 1625 and shortly afterwards began striking coins in his own name. Owing to the civil strife that England suffered whilst Charles was on the throne, the numismatic history of the period is rather complicated. The principal mint was the Tower, but during the Civil War period from 1642 until 1649, mints were variously set up at Aberystwyth

(1638–42), York (1642–4), Shrewsbury (October to December 1642), Truro (November 1642–September 1643), Oxford (1642–6), Bristol (1643–5), Combe Martin (1645–8), Exeter (September 1643–April 1646), Weymouth (1643–4), Salisbury or Sandsfoot Castle (1644), Chester (1644), Scarborough (1644–5), Carlisle (October 1644–May 1645), Lundy Island and/or Appledore and Barnstaple (1645–6), Worcester (1646), Newark (1645–6), Colchester (June–August 1648) and Pontefract (June 1648–March 1649).

Charles's coins struck during the early part of his reign do not differ greatly from those of his father. The king's bust now faces left instead of right and on many of the coins the value in Roman numerals is placed behind the king's head thus: V on the gold crown, XII on the shilling and II on the half-groat. In 1625 Nicholas Briot brought to England the latest French machinery and together with the mill and screw presses used in Elizabeth's reign produced a number of very handsome patterns for coins. The coin illustrated on PLATE VII, 7, is a pattern threepence by Briot, struck in 1634 at the Tower mint. Unfortunately, these were never issued for circulation, but other coins produced from dies engraved by him and struck from his machinery were issued and they make a very welcome addition to the English series.

The Civil War period in which the king was forced to flee from London in 1642 presents an unusual and bewildering variety of coins, particularly those struck at the besieged Royalist towns of Carlisle, Colchester, Newark, Pontefract and Scarborough. The interest of this particular issue lies in the fact that owing to the shortage of proper minting facilities, the coins were struck out of odd shaped pieces of plate which were simply hammered flat and then struck with the dies. Apparently little attempt was made to strike coins of a uniform denomination as the values of the coins struck depend on the weight of the pieces of silver used. Thus we have some rather odd denominations struck at Scarborough such as 2*s* 2*d*, 1*s* 3*d*, 11*d* and 7*d*—all of these coins are rare. The commonest of the siege pieces are of Newark and Pontefract although the specimen illustrated on PLATE VII, 6, is a rarity struck in the name of Charles II after the death of Charles I.

Apart from the siege pieces, other notable additions to the coinage were the large silver pounds and half-pounds which were struck at some of the provincial mints. These pound pieces, which measure 2 in. in diameter and weigh some 3¾ oz., are the largest silver coins in the English series.

After the execution of Charles I in 1649 Parliament struck coins in the name of the Commonwealth of England and this again provides us with another phenomenon in that the legends were in English instead of the usual Latin. Both gold and silver coins were struck; and the issue consisted of gold units, double-crowns and crowns; and silver crowns (PLATE VIII, 1), half-crowns, shillings, sixpences, twopences, pennies and halfpennies. All the coins with the exception of the halfpenny (which has a single shield on each side) have the shield of St George on the obverse and the combined shields of St George and Ireland on the other.

In 1653 Oliver Cromwell became Protector of England and a new series of coins was struck. These had been designed by one of England's most outstanding engravers, Thomas Simon, and the portrait of Cromwell is a good if unflattering one—even reproducing the wart on the Protector's chin. The inscription on the obverse reads OLIVAR·D·G·R·P·ANG·SCO·HIB &c PRO (Oliver, by the Grace of God, Protector of the Republic of England, Scotland and Ireland, etc.). Seven denominations were issued, three in gold and four in silver consisting of the gold fifty-shillings, broad (20s), half-broad (10s); and the silver crown, half-crown, shilling and sixpence.

In 1634 Lord Maltravers had purchased from the Duchess of Richmond, widow of the Duke of Lennox, the licence to strike copper farthings originally granted to Lord Harrington by James I and when the issue of 'Maltravers' farthings was stopped in 1644, another shortage of small change occurred. Although several patterns for farthings had been struck, none were ever issued and consequently the shopkeepers again began to issue their own private tokens. Large numbers of these were issued representing almost every conceivable occupation and a collection of these presents an extremely interesting insight into the life of the population at this period.

During the reign of Charles II commencing in 1660 the English coinage underwent one of the most important changes in its history; the final relinquishing of hand-produced coins in favour of coins produced by machinery. Hammered coins continued to be produced until 1662 when Pierre Blondeau began to strike the new coins with his machinery.

Four denominations of gold coins were issued—the five guineas, two guineas, guinea and half-guinea. The name 'guinea' is derived from gold supplied by the Africa Company which operated on the Guinea Coast. Coins made from this gold have the Company's badge, an elephant or an elephant and castle below the king's bust (PLATE VIII, 3). Some silver coins were struck bearing this badge on them, produced from silver also supplied by the Africa Company. Other marks of this nature are found on some of the silver coins: a plume denoting that the silver was obtained from mines in Wales and a rose signifying that it came from mines in the west of England. A regal copper coinage was introduced at long last and Charles thus effectively put an end to the private tokens that were still being produced. The issue consisted of halfpennies and farthings with a laureate bust of Charles facing left and the inscription CAROLVS A CAROLO (Charles from [son of] Charles). The reverse bears the seated figure of Britannia holding a shield and a spear in one hand and an olive branch in the other. Tradition has it that the model for this was Frances, duchess of Richmond. Farthings in tin of a similar design to the copper ones were struck in 1684 in an attempt to save money, due to copper having to be imported from Sweden. The issue was not a successful one, however, and they were only struck in the one year.

This reign also saw special coins struck for the first time for distribution at the Maundy ceremony. It had long been the custom for the sovereign to perform an act of humility by washing the feet of a number of the poor in memory of Christ washing the feet of his disciples. This act was performed on Maundy Thursday, the Thursday before Easter, the sovereign also distributing alms in the form of food, clothing and money. Until about 1800 silver pennies were the only coins struck for distribution at the Maundy ceremony although silver twopences, threepences and fourpences were struck for general circulation and are usually classed as being Maundy Money together with the pennies. From 1800, however, all of the denominations from the fourpence to the penny seem to have been intended for use at the Maundy ceremony. It is interesting to note that these unusual little coins are still struck today and are in fact the only coins in our so-called 'silver' coinage still being struck in that metal; the fineness is 925 parts in 1,000.

James II who succeeded his brother Charles reigned for just less than four years and his only interesting contribution to the coinage was the issue of the so-called 'gun-money' struck in Ireland. These were struck after William of Orange (later William III) had forced James to abdicate and the latter fled to Ireland where he endeavoured to raise an army to regain the throne. Money was short, however, and in order to pay his troops James had to melt up old cannon and church bells and turn them into coins. They are struck in brass and are particularly interesting because of their being the only British coins to be dated with the month as well as the year of issue.

William III and his wife Mary were crowned in Westminster Cathedral on 13 February 1689 and until Mary died of smallpox in 1694, their conjoined busts are depicted on the coins. Three different reverse designs were used on the half-crowns; the first type struck in 1689 consists of a crowned shield with the arms of England, Scotland, Ireland and France quarterly with the rampant lion of Orange-Nassau in an inescutcheon in the centre. The second shield used in 1689 and again in 1690 has the arms of England and France quarterly in the first and fourth quarters with the arms of Scotland and Ireland in the second and third quarters. From 1691 to 1693 a design of cruciform shields was used with the monogram WM and the date thus 1/6/9/3 in between. Other denominations retain the same type throughout.

After the death of Mary, only William's head appears on the coins. PLATE VIII, 2, illustrates the highest denomination of the reign, the gold five guineas. The badge of the Africa Company is again found on the gold coins as are the roses and plumes on the silver. Copper halfpennies and farthings were also issued.

Although milled coins had been struck since 1662, many of the old 'hammered' coins were still in circulation and in 1695 it was decided to demonetize all those remaining in circulation and replace them with new coins. In order to help the Tower mint during the re-coinage, mints were set up at Bristol, Chester, Exeter, Norwich and York and coins minted at these centres can be distinguished by the letters B. C. E. N and Y respectively below the king's bust.

The coinage of Queen Anne is of particular interest since it was during her reign (in 1707) that the kingdoms of England and Scotland were united, an act which is commemorated on the coins by the English and Scottish arms being placed side by side in one shield. The coins issued during the reign can therefore be divided into two periods: those struck before the Union in 1707 and those struck after it. Coins issued during the first period simply bear the arms of England, Scotland, France and Ireland in cruciform shields whilst those issued after 1707 have the English and Scottish arms side by side as previously mentioned (PLATE VIII, 4). Some of the silver after-Union coins were struck at the Edinburgh mint and a small E or E* is placed below the bust to denote this.

The coinage of Anne is also of interest for those coins that have the word VIGO below the bust. Coins bearing this name were struck from bullion captured by an Anglo-Dutch expedition under the command of the Duke of Ormond and Lord Rooke who sailed against the Spanish in 1702 and sacked the towns of Cadiz and Vigo. At the latter they captured several galleons and treasure to the value of some 11,000,000 pieces of eight. Large quantities of silver coins were struck from this silver and some gold coins too have the VIGO inscription; these latter are rare, however.

CHAPTER NINE

England IV

Hanover to House of Windsor

On the death of Queen Anne in 1714 the crown was offered to George Louis, elector of Hanover, and on his accession to the English throne he placed his German titles on some of the English coins. These somewhat lengthy titles are abbreviated as follows: GEORGIUS.DG.M.B.FR.ET.HIB.REX.FD. and continue on the reverse BRVN.ET.L.DVX.S.R.I.A.TH.ET.EL meaning 'George, by the Grace of God, King of Great Britain, France and Ireland, Defender of the Faith, Duke of Brunswick and Lüneburg, Arch Treasurer and Elector of the Holy Roman Empire'. The royal arms on the coins were also changed so that the Hanoverian arms could be included in the fourth quarter.

On some crowns, half-crowns, shillings and sixpences struck in 1723, the letters SSC were placed in the angles of the cross on the reverse. This was to denote that the silver was brought to the mint by the South Sea Company of 'South Sea Bubble' fame. Two other companies supplied silver to the mint, the 'Welsh Copper Company' whose initials WCC were placed below the king's bust and the 'Company for smelting down Lead with Pitcoale and Seacoale', denoted by roses and plumes in the angles of the cross on the reverse (PLATE VIII, 5).

Halfpennies and farthings were again issued between 1717 and 1724. Halfpennies issued in 1717 and 1718 and farthings issued in 1717 were struck on a rather dumpy flan whereas later issues have a large one.

Coins struck from captured Spanish bullion were again issued in 1745 and 1746. These have the word LIMA below the bust of George II indicating that the bullion was provided by Admiral Anson mainly from a captured Spanish plate ship, the "Nuestra Senora de Covadonga" encountered en route from Acapulco to Manila.

The coins struck during the reign of George II, generally speaking, may be divided into two types, those bearing a youthful portrait of the king and those struck later with an older head.

Gold coins from the five guineas to the half-guinea, together with the silver from the crown to the sixpence were struck with both portraits. The halfpennies and farthings also bear both portraits but on the Maundy Money the portrait does not change and retains the young bust throughout.

George III succeeded his grandfather in 1760 and during his long reign several innovations were made in the coinage. The highest denomination to be struck was the guinea; patterns for five and two-guinea pieces were struck but no specimens were issued for circulation. Third-guineas were struck for the first time in 1797 and again an issue of quarter-guineas (the last had been made in 1718 under George I) was made in 1762 but the denomination was not a success and was only issued in the one year. Two new copper coins were also struck. Copper twopences and pennies dated 1797 were struck by Matthew Boulton on a steam press produced in collaboration with James Watt, the inventor of the steam engine. These coins, weighing two ounces and one ounce respectively, were so expertly produced that forgery of them was made virtually impossible. Pennies and halfpennies of a different design were again issued in 1806 and 1807.

Between 1775 and 1797 no copper coins were struck at all and again the private traders and industries took it upon themselves to produce their own tokens to alleviate the difficult situation. Vast numbers of these eighteenth-century tokens were produced, many of them being made payable in more than one city and many of them were not in fact genuine traders' tokens at all, but were produced for collectors, the collecting of coins being rather fashionable at this time. Following the issue of copper coins in 1807, the price of copper became high and prevented Boulton from obtaining it at an economic figure. Again, therefore, copper tokens made their appearance in 1811 with legends such as ONE PENNY PAYABLE AT BILSTON/BRADLEY BILSTON & PRIESTFIELD. COLLIERIES & IRON WORKS, reflecting the growth of industry during the early nineteenth century.

One of the commonest gold coins of the reign of George III is the 'spade' guinea. These coins, struck between 1787 and 1799 are so named because of the spade-like shield that is used as the reverse design. Many brass counters exist, made in imitation of the spade guinea, and bear such inscriptions as IN MEMORY OF THE GOOD OLD DAYS. These have been made for use at card games.

The age-old problem of how to prevent the export of silver to the Continent was by no means settled in the eighteenth and nineteenth centuries and to alleviate the critical shortage of silver coins the mint decided in 1797 to buy a quantity of Spanish eight-real pieces and to counter-stamp them with a punch bearing the head of George III. The fact that these pieces were lighter than the English crown and circulated at 4s 9d gave rise to the saying, 'two king's heads not worth a crown'. Later, when the price of silver rose, these countermarked dollars were revalued at 5s and it was decided not to continue countermarking the Spanish coins but to overstrike them with an entirely new design, the coin being known as the Bank of England dollar (PLATE IX, 1).

In 1816, in order to straighten out the somewhat complicated situation, it was decided to have a re-coinage. The Royal Mint was re-equipped with the new steam-powered machinery and moved from its cramped quarters in the Tower to a new site on Tower Hill. The gold coinage was revalued and coins to the value of 20s and its fractions instead of 21s were struck. These new coins were called sovereigns. Patterns for five-and two-pound pieces were struck but were never adopted and the sovereign issued between 1817 and 1820, together with the half-sovereign, became the highest denominations issued. The silver crown was not struck until 1818 but half-crowns, shillings and sixpences of the new design had been struck since 1816 and were struck each year until the death of the king in 1820.

A pattern for a five-pound piece was produced during the reign of George IV but the design was never adopted. Two-pound pieces were, however, issued together with sovereigns and half-sovereigns.

Silver coins of the same denominations as the previous reign were again issued, together with the Maundy Money which was struck in every year with the exception of 1821. Pennies, half-pennies and farthings were also coined and also two new denominations, copper half- and third-farthings. These, strictly speaking, are not English coins as they were intended for use in the colonies, the half-farthings being struck in 1828 and 1830 and the third-farthings only in 1827.

George IV was an unpopular king; during his early years he had been strictly disciplined, a fact which no doubt led him into the somewhat tortuous romantic intrigues in which he became involved. Despite the fact that he was commonly called the 'first gentleman of Europe', news of his death was received by many people with some feelings of relief and during subsequent reigns his extravagances were remembered with disgust. A rather amusing rhyme composed in 1855 seems to sum up the general feeling at the time:

> George the First was always reckoned
> Vile, but viler George the Second;
> And what mortal ever heard
> Any good of George the Third?
> When from earth the Fourth descended,
> God be praised, the Georges ended!

William IV, 'the sailor King', altered the coinage but little from his predecessor. The largest gold coin, the two-pound piece, was never issued for circulation and only appears in the proof sets of 1831. The crown too, only appears as a proof, but some specimens turn up in rather worn condition nowadays, indicating that they may have slipped into circulation by mistake. Owing to the fact that the crown completes a 'type' set of crown pieces for the collector of English coins, it is now a much sought after coin and commands a high price.

Groats (fourpenny pieces) bearing the figure of Britannia seated, were struck in 1836 and 1837 and continued to be struck with the same design during the early years of Victoria's reign.

Half- and third-farthings were again struck for use in the colonies together with a new coin, the three-halfpence, that first appeared in 1834. This latter coin was only struck between 1834 and 1837 during William's reign, but was also issued between 1838 and 1843 and in 1860, 1862 and 1870 by Victoria.

The reign of Victoria may be divided into three periods; coins struck between 1838 and 1887, bearing the young head of the queen, from 1887 to 1893 with the 'Jubilee' head and from 1893 to 1901 with an older portrait. During the first period the highest denomination issued for circulation was the sovereign. The crown was first struck in 1839 but only as a proof and it was not until 1844 that large numbers were issued for circulation. The year 1847 saw the striking of a rather unusual coin which is a typical example of Victorian art but which is nevertheless a rather delightful coin; this was the so-called 'Gothic' crown. These coins were never issued for circulation, but a comparatively large number of proofs were struck and so examples of this coin can today be obtained at a reasonable figure. A similar design was adopted for the florin in 1851 and since the date appears on the obverse of the coin in Roman numerals, it is often thought by the uninitiated to have no date at all. The first florin had been struck in 1849 with a bust similar to that on the Gothic crown and had earned itself the name 'Godless' florin because the letters D:G: or Dei Gratia (By the Grace of God) were omitted from the design (PLATE IX, 3).

The other silver denominations together with the copper coins bear the uncrowned young head of the queen which was altered in 1887 to that of the crowned 'Jubilee' head; no copper coins were struck with this type, however. In 1860 bronze coins were introduced to replace the large copper coins which were rather clumsy and soon became worn because of the softness of the metal and the amount of circulation they received (PLATE IX, 2). The young head was maintained until 1894 on the pennies and halfpennies, 1895 on the farthings and 1885 on the third-farthings.

The obverse design for the 'Jubilee' coins was by Sir J. Boehm, the engraving for the dies being executed by L. C. Wyon who also designed the reverse. Although the general design for the obverse is a good one, the result is spoilt by an over-small crown balanced none too securely on top of the Queen's head. Five-pound and two-pound pieces, together with sovereigns and half-sovereigns were produced in large quantities and today these are some of the commonest gold coins in the English series. *Double-florins* or four shilling pieces were struck for the first time in 1887 and continued until 1890, by which time they had become so unpopular that the issue was discontinued. The reverses used for both gold and silver during the period 1887 to 1893 did not alter with the exception of the sixpence. The original design for this coin had been the usual crowned bust of the queen on the obverse whilst the reverse bore a crowned shield. The result was a marked similarity to the half-sovereign, a fact which was noted by some unscrupulous members of the public who proceeded to gild the sixpences and pass them off as half-sovereigns. During the latter part of 1887 therefore, the reverse design was altered by putting the word sixpence within a laurel wreath.

In 1893 the Jubilee type was replaced by a portrait more suited to the queen who was now in her seventy-fourth year and depicts a much older bust wearing a coronet from which flows a long veil (PLATE IX, 4). The letters IND:IMP are also included in her titles on these coins; she had become Empress of India in 1876 but this fact had not previously been noted on the coinage.

Edward VII who succeeded Victoria in 1901 continued to issue the same denominations as his mother and no new values were struck.

George V also followed the same pattern of coinage as his predecessor but more variety of types occurs during the reign due to there being two different reverse designs for most of the coins and some slight variations in the bust on the obverse.

Following the 1914–18 war, the price of silver rose alarmingly until in 1920 the coins were worth more for the metal than their face value. Consequently a debased silver coinage containing only fifty per cent silver was issued. George V's Jubilee was celebrated in 1935 and to commemorate this a crown piece with a new design was issued. The reverse design is St George on a spirited horse rearing over a dragon. This design by Percy Metcalfe is a very modernistic one and has earned little admiration from collectors (PLATE IX, 5).

Some of the pennies struck in 1912 have a small H in the exergue, whilst some dated 1918 and 1919 have a small H or KN on them; this denotes that they were struck by either Messrs Heaton & Co., or the Kings Norton Copper Company.

After the death of George V in January 1936 new dies were prepared for the coinage of Edward VIII. It is believed that a few of the twelve-sided threepenny pieces were sent to slot machine manufacturers to obtain their comments on this coin, the shape of which was new to the English coinage and a very few of these were not returned to the mint and have since got into the hands of collectors.

Edward VIII coins struck for the various Commonwealth countries (East and West Africa, Fiji and New Guinea) are quite common. Since these coins are pierced with a centre hole there is naturally no portrait of Edward on them.

The coins issued by George VI were originally struck in fifty per cent silver but in 1947 the coinage was debased still further to its present composition of cupro-nickel. One other important change took place in the reign: this was the relinquishing of the title Emperor of India in 1947 which title was therefore subsequently omitted from the inscription on the coins in 1949.

Sets of gold coins consisting of proof five- and two-pound pieces together with sovereigns and half-sovereigns were issued in 1937. Proof sets of the silver and copper coins were also issued in this year. Two types of shilling were struck; the English type with the royal lion standing on a crown and the Scottish type, issued as a compliment to the queen's Scottish ancestry, which has the Scottish lion seated facing holding a sword in one paw and the sceptre in the other.

The crown piece was only struck in two years—1937 and 1951, the latter being in commemoration of the Festival of Britain—a national exhibition of British achievements and industry. It also commemorated the centenary of the great exhibition of 1851 and incidentally the four hundredth anniversary of the introduction of the silver crown into the British coinage. The edge of the coin is lettered and reads MDCCCLI CIVIUM INDUSTRIA FLORET CIVITAS MCMLI (1851 By the industry of its people the State flourishes 1951).

In the reign of our present queen, only two types have as yet appeared. In 1954 the words BRITT: OMN were omitted from the coins since they were considered as not being entirely in keeping with the modern conception of royalty. Both English and Scottish types of shillings have been issued each year and two crown pieces have also been struck; the coronation crown of 1953, the obverse type of which is reminiscent of the first crown of Edward VI since the queen is depicted as an equestrian figure. The crown dated 1960 reverts to the customary profile of the queen's head. With the exception of sovereigns (PLATE IX, 6) struck in 1957, '58 and '59 as part of a £10,000,000 order from the Treasury, no other gold coins have been struck during the reign of Elizabeth II. The reverse of these coins bears the St George and dragon design which was originally produced by Pistrucci for the 1818 crown.

CHAPTER TEN

Scotland and Ireland

Scotland
Compared with the long history of English numismatics, the Scottish series covers a relatively short period from the twelfth to the eighteenth century. Recent research has now definitely attributed the earliest Scottish coins, which were silver pennies or *stirlings*, to the reign of David I (1124–53); in appearance they are markedly similar to coins issued by the English king Stephen with whom David was contemporary. The obverse depicts the crowned head of the king facing to the right with a sceptre in front of him, together with the legend DAVIT REX. The reverse bears a cross surrounded by the name of the mint and moneyer. Stirlings of a similar type were also struck by David's son Henry, earl of Northumberland; a new type with a facing bust of the king was, however, introduced by David's successor Malcolm IV.

Perhaps the commonest of the early coins are those pennies (for this they may now be called) of the second coinage of Alexander III (1249–86) which were struck in very large quantities. These bear the bust of the king facing left with the customary sceptre in front, surrounded by his name and titles. The legend is continued on the reverse, the central design of which is a long cross extending to the edge of the coin. It was this king too, who coined halfpennies and farthings for the first time, the design being similar to that of the penny.

The first gold coins of Scotland were issued by David II (1329–71), who succeeded his father Robert Bruce, well known for his defeat of the English at the battle of Bannockburn in 1314. These gold coins were called nobles and were struck in imitation of the English noble of Edward III. Their issue, however, was shortlived and they are now extremely rare, gold coins not becoming a regular part of the Scottish coinage until the reign of Robert III, some twenty years later. David was also responsible for the introduction of groats and half-groats; these are quite common.

Many attractive gold coins have been struck in the Scottish series, but perhaps the most delightful of them all are the *riders* and *unicorns* of James III. The former depicts the equestrian figure of the king wearing armour, galloping to the right and brandishing a sword, whilst the latter bears an admirable representation of that mythical animal, the unicorn, holding the shield of Scotland in its forepaws.

The reign of James V (1513–42), father of Mary Queen of Scots, is noteworthy for the abandoning of the medieval style and the emergence of a genuine attempt at portraiture. The gold coins of this reign, which bear the best portraits, are unfortunately rare, but the groats, which also have pleasing portraits on them, can occasionally be found in a reasonable state of preservation.

Billon *bawbees* equal to sixpence were produced in this reign for the first time, the obverse design being a crowned thistle between I and 5 and the reverse a St Andrew's cross through a crown.

The fact that Mary, Queen of Scots was married to François II of France has already been noted in a preceding chapter. The marriage was of short duration, however, for in December 1561 François died of an abscess in his ear, an event which prompted John Knox to write, 'Lo, the potent hand of God from above sent unto us a wonderful and most joyful deliverance. For unhappy Francis, husband to our sovereign, suddenly perisheth of a rotten ear—that deaf ear that never would hear the truth of God.' Subsequently, in 1565, Mary married Henry, Lord Darnley, but in two years she was again a widow for in 1567 Darnley was murdered. The house in Edinburgh where he was lying sick was blown up and his naked body was found lying in the garden.

These unhappy events in Mary's life are reflected in the coinage which may be divided into five main periods; that prior to her marriage to François in 1558; the period of her marriage from 1558 to 1561 (the coins may again be divided into those issued 1558–60 when François was dauphin and those struck in 1560–1 when he was king); the first widowhood of 1561–5; the period of her marriage to Darnley 1565–7 and her second widowhood which lasted only a few months.

The year 1603 saw the accession of Mary's son James to the English throne and the Scottish coinage underwent several alterations incorporating his new title; the arms of England are also now placed in the second and third quarters of the shield. From this time on until the cessation of the Scottish coinage at the union of the two kingdoms in 1707, many of the Scottish coins are similar to the English, although in some cases the Scottish thistle is used as a reverse design. An unusual feature of some of the later milled coins is the incorporation of the value in the design.

Ireland

The early numismatic history of Ireland is shrouded in uncertainty. The coinage seems to begin *circa* A.D. 1000 when the Vikings who had settled in the country around Dublin began to strike coins in imitation of the pennies of Aethelred II of England. The bust that appears on the obverse is usually crudely executed and the legends often include the name of Sihtric Anlafsson. Later issues become very much more crude so that by the middle of the eleventh century the legends are practically indecipherable.

It was not until after John became Lord of Ireland in 1177 that a better executed coinage was produced; halfpennies and farthings were struck and following John's accession to the English throne pennies were produced in the early years of the thirteenth century. Henry VI (1422–61) was responsible for the issue of the first coin of a higher denomination, the groat, which appeared in 1460. This bears no legend on the obverse, simply a large crown within a tressure of arcs, an unusual design for so large a coin; the reverse bears a long cross extending to the edge of the coin with pellets in its angles and the legend CIVI/TAS/DUBL/INIE. Another unusual coin, this time issued by Edward IV was the *double-groat* or eightpence; examples of this are rare and are seldom found in good condition.

Henry VII succeeded to the throne in 1485 and immediately began to strike Irish coins in his own name. The following year, however, the Yorkist party in Ireland pinned their fortunes on Lambert Simnel, offering him to the people in the north of England as 'Edward VI'. A number of rare groats and pennies of a similar type to those of Edward IV and a groat of Henry VII with the 'h' below the name altered to an 'E' have now been tentatively attributed to Lambert Simnel.

The coinage of Henry VIII is of particular interest since on some of the groats and half-groats, reference is made to three of Henry's wives; Katherine of Aragon, Anne Boleyn and Jane Seymour; the initials 'h k', 'h A' or 'h I' appear on the reverse.

Copper had occasionally been used as a coining medium for

Irish coins since the reign of Henry VI but the coins thus produced were only of a very limited number and the first extensive use of this metal came in the reign of Elizabeth when large quantities of pennies and halfpennies were produced.

Charles I also made use of copper to some extent but his reign is characterized by the large amount of crudely struck 'money of necessity' that was produced at Dublin.

Without doubt some of the most unusual (but also the most common) Irish coins is the 'gunmoney' already referred to (p. 87). Since that time, with the exception of a quantity of copper coins struck during the reign of the four Georges and a series of silver Bank of Ireland tokens, little coinage has been produced specially for Ireland.

With the inception of the Irish Free State in 1928 a coinage of silver, nickel and copper was produced ranging from the half-crown down to the farthing, each denomination taking for its reverse design a living creature such as a horse, a salmon or a woodcock. In 1939 the name of the country, Saorstat Eireann, was changed to Eire and the coinage was altered accordingly. The silver half-crown, shilling, and sixpence were debased from silver to cupro-nickel in 1951.

CHAPTER ELEVEN

North America

THE early settlers of the North American continent at first had little need of struck coins, all transactions being conducted by a form of barter. As life in the new colonies became more complicated, however, and traders began to arrive from overseas bringing their goods to sell, some form of currency became necessary. Since the English government did not, at the time, provide the colonists with a coinage of their own, many types of coins were used to pay these traders, English, French, Dutch and Spanish currency being particularly prevalent in the ports along the eastern seaboard. Spanish dollars or eight-real pieces, together with their fractions, struck at the mints of Mexico City and Lima in New Spain were by far the most popular of all the coins to be found in circulation and were readily acceptable. It is upon these 'pieces of eight' that the subsequent coinage of the United States was based, the two pillars with their entwined mottoes on the reverse of the coin being thought to be the origin of the dollar sign. Throughout the colonial period of American history the Spanish dollars remained the principal form of currency and it was not until 1857 that these coins were officially demonetized.

Apart from the foreign coins that circulated, payment was made in many other forms, the most general being 'wampum' or strings of shells as used by the Indians. In 1637, 'It was ordered that wampamege should passe at 6 a penny for any summe under 12*d*', and again, in 1640, 'It is ordered that white wampamege shall passe at 4 a penny and blewe at 2 a penny and not above 12*D* at any time except the receiver desire more'. In addition to wampum, musket bullets 'of a full bore shall passe currently for a farthing apeece, provided that noe man be compelled to take above XII*d*., att a tyme in them'. Horses, sheep, pigs, goats, asses, furs, grain and fish were also readily exchanged. The circulation of these articles was by no means restricted to the seventeenth and eighteenth centuries for in 1840 the marriage fee in Iowa was three goatskins or four bushels of sweet potatoes.

The earliest coins to be struck for the colonies in the Americas were those struck in the early seventeenth century for Somers Islands or the Bermudas as they are now called. These coins, made of brass and then silvered, are now extremely rare. They were known as 'hog money', the name supposedly being invented after Sir George Somers had discovered the islands to be overrun with these animals when he was shipwrecked there whilst on his way to Virginia in 1609. The first coins to be struck on the mainland were those for the New England settlements of Massachusetts. In 1652, the General Court of Massachusetts ordered one John Hull to strike a quantity of silver shillings, sixpences and threepences. The design was crude; the letters NE in script capitals in a small rectangle are on one side and the value in Roman numerals is in a similar stamp on the other. The pure simplicity of the design invited counterfeiting and the design was later radically altered to a more complicated one. The obverse of the coins bears the words MASATHVSETS IN. (or variants) around either a willow, oak or pine tree within a beaded circle and the reverse NEW ENGLAND ANO DOM (or variants) around the date and value. In the latter half of the eighteenth century some copper cents and half cents were issued with an Indian standing holding a bow and arrow on the obverse and an eagle on the reverse (PLATE X, 4). These were dated 1787 or 1788 and in the following year the mint was finally closed as being unprofitable.

In 1632 a charter was granted to Cecil, second Lord Baltimore, making him 'Lord Proprietor of Maryland' and although this charter did not specifically state that he was given coining rights, in 1658 he issued a small quantity of silver shillings, sixpences and groats together with a few pattern *denarii* or pennies in copper. All of these denominations are rare, there being only three examples known of the penny.

The silver coins have the arms of the Baltimore family on the reverse whilst the penny has a ducal coronet with two pennants flying. All of the coins depict the bust of Lord Baltimore on the obverse together with the legend 'CÆ CILIVS:DNS:TERRÆ–MARIÆ; & CT'. The dies for these coins were cut in London and a number of specimens struck and shipped out to the colony where they were readily accepted.

A rather strange series of coins next claims our attention; these are the St Patrick's or Mark Newby coins attributed to New Jersey. In November 1681, together with other immigrants from

Dublin, Mark Newby and his family arrived in New Jersey and brought with them a quantity of these copper coins. Because of the figure of St Patrick on the obverse of these pieces they are usually known as St Patrick's halfpence (PLATE X, 1). Two different sizes and designs of these coins are known; the larger, which is generally accepted as being a halfpenny, depicts St Patrick blessing a number of people together with the legend ECCE GREX (Behold the flock). The smaller piece, a farthing, again depicts St Patrick, this time casting out a large number of reptiles and animals; the legend is QVIESCAT PLEBS (May the people be quiet). Both of these denominations have the same reverse, that of a king kneeling holding an Irish harp below a crown and the legend FLOREAT REX (May the King prosper). It is thought that these coins were struck in Dublin in 1678 but this is by no means certain. What is certain, however, is that Newby must have brought a very large quantity with him for in an Act dated 8 May, 1682, they were made current in New Jersey 'and after the said eighteenth instant, pass for half-pence current of the province . . . provided also that no Person or Persons be hereby obliged to take more than five shillings in one payment'.

The shortage of coins in the colonies had long been a matter of some inconvenience to the settlers, and the English government was never very helpful regarding the striking of coins to alleviate these difficulties. In the early eighteenth century, therefore, it became necessary to import large quantities of copper coins from England and Ireland. In July 1722 William Wood obtained a patent from George I whereby he was given the right to strike 300 tons of copper coins for use in the American colonies. The arrangement was that the first 200 tons were to be struck within the first four years and not more than ten tons a year for the next ten years. The first coins were undated but subsequent issues were dated 1722 and 1723. There were three denominations, twopences, pennies and halfpennies. One type has an obverse with the head of George I facing right with his titles and a full blown rose on the reverse surrounded by the legend ROSA AMERICANA 1722 UTILE DULCI (American Rose, the useful with the pleasant). The coins were made of Bath metal, a mixture of silver, brass and tutanaigne and are believed to have been struck in London and Bristol; later some dies were allegedly taken to New York.

PLATE IX – ENGLISH

1 GEORGE III
Bank of England silver dollar, 1804.
2 VICTORIA
Copper penny, 1860.
3 VICTORIA
Silver 'godless' florin, 1849.
4 VICTORIA
Silver shilling, 1900. 'Old head' type.
5 GEORGE V
Silver crown, 1935 (reverse only). Commemorating the silver jubilee of His Majesty's reign.
6 ELIZABETH II
Gold sovereign, 1958.

PLATE X – AMERICAN

1 'ST PATRICK'S'
Copper halfpenny. St Patrick blessing populace. *Rev.* King seated, holding harp.
2 'WOOD'S'
Copper halfpenny, second issue. Head of George I, right. *Rev.* Hibernia seated, leaning on harp.
3 CONTINENTAL CURRENCY
Pewter dollar. Sundial, etc. and CONTINENTAL CURRENCY 1776. *Rev.* Linked circles, etc.
4 MASSACHUSETTS
Copper cent, 1788. Indian standing, etc. *Rev.* Eagle above date, etc.
5 UNITED STATES
Silver half-dime, 1795. Head of Liberty, right. *Rev.* Eagle within, wreath.
6 UNITED STATES
Copper cent, 1793. Head of Liberty, right. *Rev.* Value within chain.

PLATE XI – AMERICAN

1 UNITED STATES
Gold ten dollars, 1797. Head of Liberty right, wearing cap. *Rev.* Heraldic eagle below clouds and stars.

2 UNITED STATES
Gold five dollars, 1807. Bust of Liberty, left, wearing cap. *Rev.* Eagle with outstretched wings, left, value below.
3 UNITED STATES
Silver quarter dollar, 1821. Bust of Liberty, left wearing cap. *Rev.* Eagle above value.
4 UNITED STATES
Silver half-dollar, 1920, commemorating the landing of the Pilgrims at Plymouth, Mass. Pilgrim standing left. *Rev.* the 'Mayflower'.
5 UNITED STATES
Silver half-dollar, 1937, commemorating the colonization of Roanoke Island. Head of Sir Walter Raleigh, left. *Rev.* Figures commemorating the birth of Virginia Dare.

PLATE XII – CANADIAN

1 CANADA, Province
Copper 'Bouquet' sou (1837).
2 CANADA, French Régime
Billon marque, 1741. Strasbourg mint.
3 CANADA, Province
Copper halfpenny, 1842, issued by the Bank of Montreal.
4 CANADA, Province
Silver twenty cents, 1858.
5 NEWFOUNDLAND
Silver twenty cents, 1904. Heaton's mint.
6 CANADA, Dominion
Gold five dollars, 1914.
7 CANADA, Dominion
Nickel five cents, 1951. Bicentenary of the isolation of nickel.
8 NEWFOUNDLAND
Gold two dollars, 1882. Heaton's mint.

PLATE XIII – CENTRAL AND SOUTH AMERICAN

1 BOLIVIA
Silver 'cob' eight reales, 1676. Potosi mint.
2 BOLIVIA, Republic
Gold escudo, 1853, Potosi mint. Head of Simon Bolivar to right. *Rev.* Sun behind mountain and llama.
3 MEXICO
Charles and Joanna, 1519–55. Silver four reales. Mexico city mint. Crowned arms etc. *Rev.* Two pillars crowned dividing PLUS ULTRA.

Plate IX.

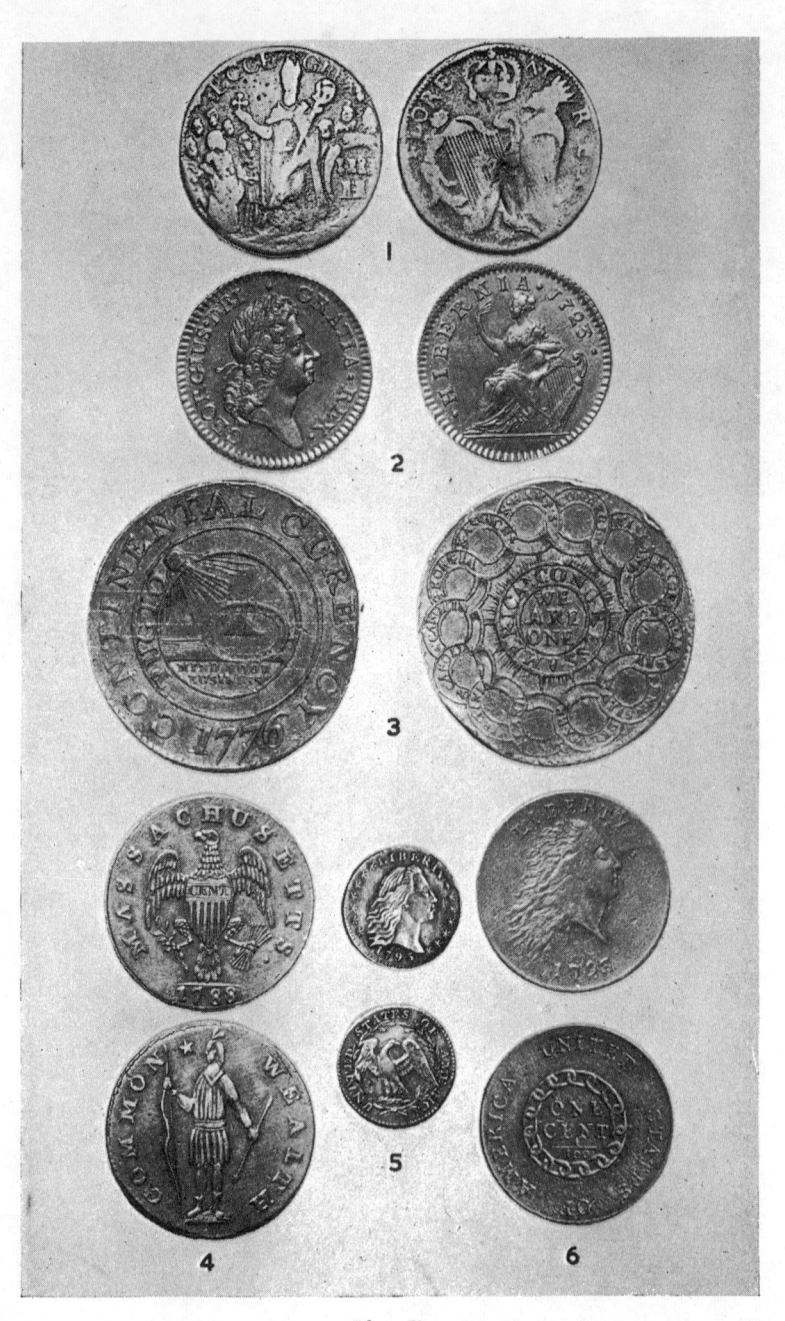

Plate X.

Plate XI.

Plate XII.

Plate XIII.

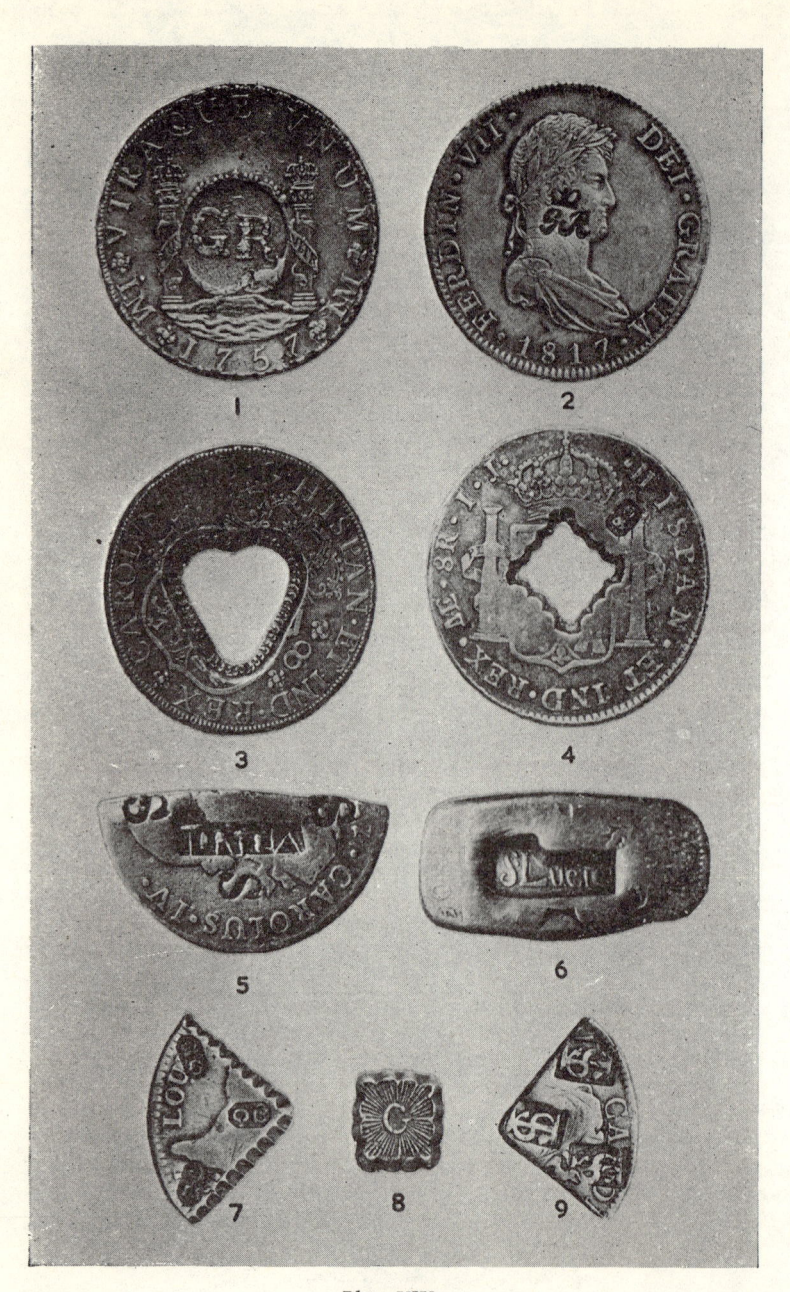

Plate XIV.

Plate XV.

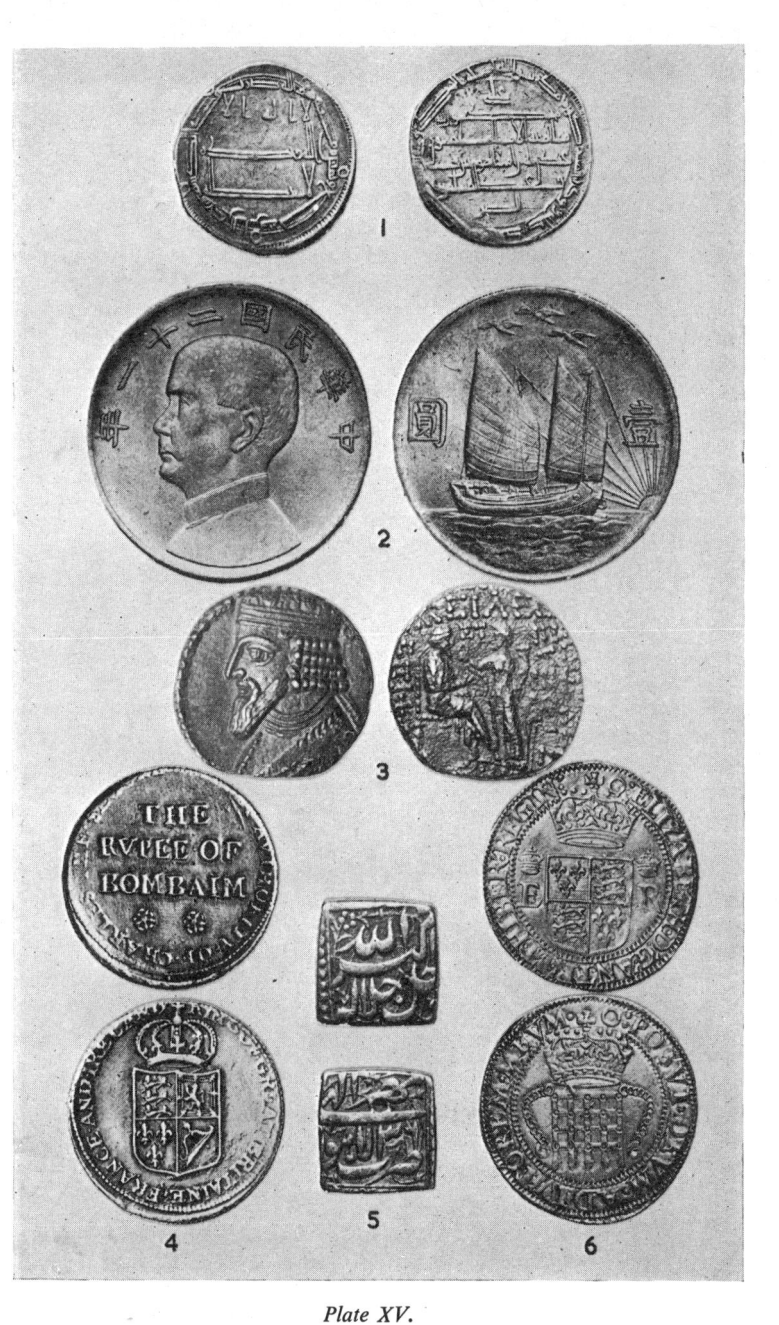

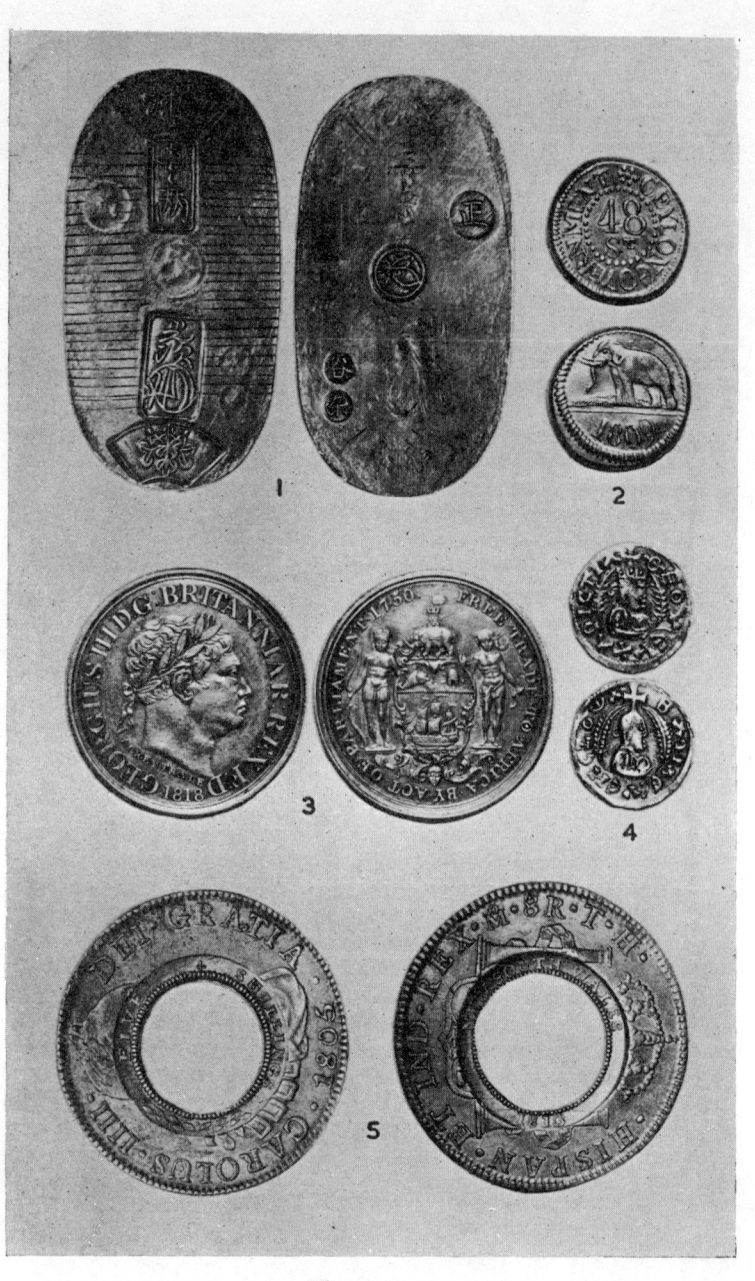

Plate XVI.

4 BRAZIL, Republic
  Silver 2,000 reis, 1932, commemorating the fourth centenary of the colonization of Brazil. Bust of John III of Portugal to right.
5 MEXICO, Republic
  Silver 5 pesos, 1955. Head of Hidalgo to left.
6 URUGUAY, Republic
  Silver peso, 1942. Head of Artigas to right.

PLATE XIV – WEST INDIAN

1 JAMAICA
  Countermarked eight reales, 1757, Lima mint. GR in capitals.
2 JAMAICA
  Countermarked eight reales, 1817, Mexico City mint. Crowned script *GR*.
3 MARTINIQUE
  Cut eight reales, 1768, Mexico City mint.
4 GUADELOUPE
  Cut and counterstamped eight reales, 1794, Lima mint. Rectangular hole with crenellations and counterstamped with crowned G. Current for nine livres.
5 TORTOLA & THE SAINTS
  Half segment of eight reales 18??. Counterstamped TORTOLA and s repeated three times.
6 ST LUCIA
  Central portion of eight reales, 1805. Countermarked S. LUCIE. Current for nine escalins.
7 GUADELOUPE
  Quarter segment of French écu. Countermarked with crowned G repeated three times. Current for two livres five sous.
8 GUADELOUPE
  Centre plug from cut dollar. Countermarked with G. Current for twenty sous.
9 ST LUCIA
  Quarter segment of eight reales. Counterstamped SL three times. Current for four escalins.

PLATE XV – ASIAN

1 ABBASIDS
  Er Rashid A.D. 786–809. Silver dirhem. *Rev.* 'Town of Shash'.
2 CHINA, Republic
  Silver dollar, 1932. Bust of Sun Yat Sen to left. *Rev.* Geese flying above junk with rising sun in background.

3 PARTHIA.
Gotazes, A.D. 40–51. Silver tetradrachm dated A.D. 48/49.
4 INDIA
E.I.C. Bombay. Silver rupee, 1678. *Rev.* Crown above royal arms.
5 INDIA
Mughal Emperors. Akbar I, 1556–1605. Silver rupee, Lahore mint.
6 INDIA
Elizabeth I, 2 reales or quarter dollar, 1600. *Rev.* Crown above portcullis, etc.

PLATE XVI – AFRICAN, ASIAN, AUSTRALASIAN

1 JAPAN
Ansei era, 1859. Gold koban, bearing various stamps denoting value and era.
2 CEYLON
George III. Silver 48 stivers, 1809. *Rev.* Elephant to left, etc.
3 GOLD COAST
George III. Silver ackey, 1818. *Rev.* Arms of the African Company.
4 AXUM
Nezana, *c.* A.D. 540–5. Gold (denomination?). Bust of king to right. *Rev.* Bust to right surmounted by cross, legends in Greek on obv. and rev.
5 AUSTRALIA
'Holey Dollar', cut from eight reales of Charles IV, Mexico City mint.

At this period Ireland was also experiencing a shortage of copper coins and Wood struck a series of coins for use in that country. They proved to be unpopular, however, and were subsequently shipped out to the colonies. This issue, known as Wood's coinage, is of two types; the first type, dated 1722 with Hibernia seated facing left holding a harp in front of her, consisted both of halfpennies and farthings, the latter being extremely rare. Later in the same year the reverse was changed in that Hibernia now leans on the harp which is placed behind her (PLATE X, 2). This second issue consisted of halfpennies and farthings; the halfpennies being struck in 1722, 1723 and 1724, the farthings only in the last two years.

Following the Declaration of Independence in 1776, the state of New Hampshire considered the possibility of a copper coinage and on 13 March, 1776, the House of Representatives authorized William Moulton to strike a limited quantity of patterns for their consideration. The designs were never approved, however, and only very few of the coins ever found their way into circulation. There are three types known to exist, all of them being exceedingly rare and varying in design from a tree on the obverse to a harp on the reverse of one and the letters 'WM' on the reverse of the other.

Under the Articles of Confederation of the States adopted on 9 July, 1778, Congress was allowed to regulate the alloy and values of the coins struck by each state, who retained the right to strike their own coins. Subsequently, states such as Vermont, New York, Connecticut, and New Jersey considered striking coins and in fact large numbers of copper coins of varying types were authorized for circulation.

Apart from coins which were actually intended for circulation, various other tokens and medals which relate to this period of American history are generally classed as having been passed as currency. Not the least of these is the series of pieces that bear the portrait of George Washington on the obverse. Many varieties of these exist and they vary in date between 1783 and 1795.

In 1776 dollar-sized coins were produced, probably in New York. These are rather strange coins in appearance with a sundial as the central design on the obverse and below it the inscription MIND YOUR BUSINESS. Round this is the legend CONTINENTAL CURRENCY 1776. The reverse is devoted to a series of linked circles, each bearing the name of a state and in the centre is the motto AMERICAN CONGRESS WE ARE ONE (PLATE X, 3). These pieces were struck in three different metals, silver, brass and pewter. Those struck in pewter may be classed as scarce or rare, the silver and brass examples as extremely rare.

A series of coins that may be regarded as patterns for a coinage of the United States are the so-called 'Nova Constellatio' patterns struck in silver. They were designed by Gouverneur Morris in 1783 and are excessively rare. There are three denominations, the *Mark, Quint* and *Cent*. Based on the decimal system, the Mark was equal to 1,000 units, the Quint 500 and the cent 100, the unit (mill) being a quarter grain of silver. The obverse has the central design of an eye surrounded by rays and the legend NOVA CONSTELLATIO. The reverse is LIBERTAS JUSTITIA 1783 around a wreath in which appears U.S. and the value. These patterns had been designed for Robert Morris, head of the Confederation finance department, and in 1783 and 1785 large numbers of copper cents were struck in Birmingham based on the design of the silver Nova Constellatio patterns. The 1786 Nova Constellatio copper is believed to be a contemporary counterfeit: only a few examples are known.

On 6 July 1785 Congress passed a resolution that the national currency was to be based on the decimal system, the units being *dollars* and *cents*. In 1786 Congress authorized the first issue of copper coins—the 'fugio' cents of 1787. The coins were mainly struck in New York and New Haven, Connecticut and bore . . . 'the following device, viz., thirteen circles linked together, a small circle in the middle, with the words UNITED STATES round it, and in the centre, the words WE ARE ONE; on the other side of the same piece the following device, viz., a dial with the hours expressed on the face of it, a meridian sun above, on one side of which is to be the word FUGIO and on the other the year in figures 1787 below the dial the words MIND YOUR BUSINESS'. The copper for this coinage was obtained by one James Jarvis from military stores and it is believed that it was mainly in the form of copper bands from around powder kegs.

On 3 March 1791 Congress passed another resolution dealing with the national currency, this time definitely authorizing a mint to be set up and the president to engage artists and purchase coining machinery. It was not until 1792, however, that the first coins were struck at the new mint set up in Philadelphia These were the *half disme* (half dime) and possibly also the *disme* (dime) struck from silver plate supplied by George Washington himself. The obverse bears the head of Liberty facing left, a portrait which is thought to be modelled on Washington's wife Martha and the legend LIBERTY PARÆNT OF SCIENCE AND INDUSTRY. The reverse bears an eagle flying left and UNITED STATES OF AMERICA. The issue of these coins was very limited, however, and it was not until the following year that coins were struck in any quantity and even then the issue only consisted of cents (PLATE X, 6) and half cents.

The half cent was the lowest value ever issued by the United States. Even in those days of low prices, a half-cent piece was considered a nuisance; its coinage declined and it was discontinued altogether in 1857. The designs used were very similar to the large cents.

The one-cent piece has been the most regularly produced U.S. coin. A one-cent piece has been struck in every year except 1815. In 1793, its first year, 112,212 pieces in three different designs were issued. Because of sales taxes today and the policy of pricing merchandise at '$1.98', etc. the demand for one-cent pieces has grown so that the annual coinage currently exceeds two billion pieces.

The first cents were struck on large copper planchets, about the size of modern quarters. It was a clumsy coin to use and expensive to produce. The large cents were discontinued along with the half cents in 1857. In the same year a new type showing an eagle in flight was introduced on a small, thick planchet. The composition of these new cents was 88 per cent copper and 12 per cent nickel, thus giving the coin a rather whitish appearance. In 1859 the type was again altered, the 'flying eagle' being dropped in favour of the Indian head design. The figure actually represents Liberty decked out in a feather head-dress as the law of 1792 had specified that 'an impression emblematical of Liberty, with an inscription of the word LIBERTY, and the year of coinage' was to appear on one side of each coin. Collectors have always known these coins, however, as 'Indian head cents'. The weight was reduced and the composition altered again in 1864 to 95 per cent copper and 5 per cent tin and zinc (bronze); the design remained unchanged until 1909. In this year the familiar bust of Abraham Lincoln was placed on the obverse, where it remains to this day. Public reception of the new coin was very favourable but protests arose over the use of the designer's initials (V.D.B. for Victor D. Brenner) in a prominent position on the back of the coin. The Secretary of the Treasury ordered the initials removed from subsequent coinage. This order went into effect after only 484,000 pieces had been struck at the San Francisco mint creating one of the rarities of the series. The 1909-S VDB cent currently sells for about $150 in uncirculated condition. The reverse of the Lincoln cent was redesigned in 1959 to commemorate the 150th anniversary of his birth.

The Civil War gave birth to two unusual coins, the two-cent piece and the nickel three-cent piece. The two-cent piece is memorable as being the first U.S. coin to carry the motto 'In God We Trust'. A great deal of religious sentiment had been created by the war, resulting in this legend which now appears on all coins and is being used on new paper money as well. The two-cent piece was issued from 1864 through 1873.

The three-cent nickel piece was introduced in 1865 for the redemption of paper three-cent notes that had been pressed into use during the war. Most collectors are surprised to learn that the three-cent piece was the first American 'nickel' coin. The first five-cent piece struck in nickel did not appear until the following year, 1866.

The first so-called 'nickel' was authorized in 1866. Its composition is 75 per cent copper and 25 per cent nickel and except for the wartime years of 1942/45 has been struck in this composition ever since. The first nickel bore a Federal shield on the obverse. This was changed to a head of Liberty in 1883, the Buffalo-Indian design in 1913 and, finally, the Jefferson head in use today.

The first United States silver coins were struck in 1794: dollars, halves and half dimes. The early half dimes were charming little coins and weighed only some 20 grains (PLATE X, 5). There was no mark or indication of value on these coins until 1829. In 1837 the type was changed to a seated figure of Liberty designed by Christian Gobrecht. This type was continued with a few minor variations until 1873.

The silver dime came into being in 1796. The early dimes were much the same as the silver half dimes. The head of Liberty designed by Barber was used from 1892 until 1916, followed by the Weinman design. This coin is commonly known as a 'Mercury head' dime although, like the Indian head cent it is in fact another representation of Liberty. The wings on her cap are intended to symbolize liberty of thought. The dimes issued since 1946 carry the portrait of the late President Franklin D. Roosevelt.

The shortest-lived U.S. denomination was the twenty-cent piece, regularly issued only in 1875 and 1876. (Proofs were made in 1877 and 1878.) They were too easily confused with quarters even though they had a smooth edge compared to the quarter's reeded edge.

The dollar, together with its half and quarter, are the three remaining silver denominations that were authorized as early as the eighteenth century. The dollar and half dollar first appeared in 1794 and the quarter dollar in 1796. Their designs were the same as the dime and half dime until 1916. A standing figure of Liberty was used on quarters from 1916 through 1930. The coins issued since 1932 bear the bust of George Washington. A walking figure of Liberty was used on the halves from 1916 through 1947. The design with Benjamin Franklin and the Liberty bell has been in use since 1948. No silver dollars have been struck since 1935 and with the large numbers still in the Treasury vaults it is not likely that more will be needed for many years.

The bill dated 2 April 1792 that gave birth to the coinage of the United States provided for the issue of three gold coins; the eagle of ten dollars, the half eagle and the quarter eagle. In fact it was not until three years later, in 1795, that the eagle (PLATE XI, 1) and its half first appeared and the quarter eagle was not struck until 1796. The obverse of these coins depicts a capped head of Liberty surrounded by stars with the exception of some specimens of the quarter eagle dated 1796 where no stars are shown. The reverse is devoted to an eagle in various forms with outstretched neck. Examples of these dated in the eighteenth century are exquisite coins and when in fine condition realize high prices.

The discovery of gold in California in 1848 and the subsequent gold rush in the following year were no doubt partly responsible for the issue of two new denominations in 1849. Dies were prepared for the double eagle in 1849 but only one specimen is believed to have been struck in this year and this is now in the U.S. mint collection. However, in 1850 over 1,170,000 specimens were struck and these large coins which weigh some 516 grains or equal to over four sovereigns, were struck every year with the exception of 1917, 1918 and 1919 until 1933. In that year America went off the gold standard and since then all the necessary backing for its note issue has been in the form of bullion. The issue of gold dollars was of a much shorter duration, they were only struck until 1889.

A companion piece to the unpopular silver twenty-cents may be found in the gold three dollars that was issued in 1854; these too were never widely accepted and the issue was discontinued in 1889.

The scope of this chapter does not permit any great consideration to be given to the many patterns, proofs, ingots and commemorative coins that have appeared during the short but eventual history of American numismatics. Exception must, however, be made with regard to the interesting series of commemorative half dollars. This series comprising some forty-eight types has, over the years, depicted some of the events in the history of the formation of the United States and a collection of these coins presents American history in a most instructive and interesting manner. Generally speaking, these coins were struck at the Philadelphia mint (other branch mints were used occasionally, however) and were sold at a premium by the commission who organized the commemorative events. The two specimens illustrated on PLATE XI have been selected as being typical of the series as a whole and because of their interest to readers of this book on both sides of the Atlantic. No. 4 was struck in 1920 with the authority of Congress to commemorate the landing of the Pilgrims at Plymouth in Massachusetts in 1620. No. 5 commemorates the 350th anniversary of the colonization of Roanoke Island, North Carolina, by Sir Walter Raleigh in 1587, as well as the birth of Virginia Dare, the first white child to be born on the North American continent. The coin was struck for the celebrations in Old Fort Raleigh in 1937.

CHAPTER TWELVE

Canada

CANADA was discovered in 1497 by John Cabot who, sailing under Letters Patent from Henry VII, claimed it for England. However, it was not until 1534 when the French took possession of the country, giving it the name of 'New France' that any continuous history of the country is known. In 1541 another French expedition led by M. de Robesval gave it its present name by thinking the native name for huts, 'kanata', was the name of the country. The first settlement was made at Port Royal, now Annapolis, in 1605 and subsequent settlements were made at Quebec in 1608. Despite various attempts by England to regain possession of the country it remained in French hands until 1763, when it was ceded to England by the Treaty of Paris.

During the French régime, silver coins valued at five and fifteen sols, dated 1680 and bearing the bust of Louis XIV on one side with a crowned shield on the other, circulated together with billon *marques* (PLATE XII, 2) and *half marques*. Copper twenty, twelve, nine and six deniers were struck, but only the nine deniers were actually ever circulated, the bulk of the other denominations being returned to France where they were subsequently melted down.

Much of the early numismatic history of Canada has, in fact, already been covered in the preceding chapter on North America. The same conditions prevailed—farm produce and other objects being used as a form of barter—the gradual influx of traders to the seaports necessitating some form of currency which the British Government was reluctant to supply—the varieties of foreign coins being used before a regular currency was introduced.

We have seen that belts of wampum were used as currency in America and these were also current in Canada, remaining so until about 1700; the Indians continued to accept them until the early 1800's. The Spanish-American milled dollar was also circulated at this period and Prince Edward Island provides us with one of the first examples of a 'holey dollar', i.e., a Spanish dollar with the centre punched out. Examples of this type of coin are to be found on PLATE XIV where somewhat similar specimens are illustrated that have been mutilated for use in Martinique and Guadaloupe. In the instance of the Prince Edward Island coin, the centre piece was circular and both the resultant ring and centre passed as currency, the former at five shillings and the latter at one shilling. It was soon discovered, however, that the centres were worth approximately 1s 3d, for the metal value and a large quantity of these were accumulated for shipment to England for melting. The ship carrying them was unfortunately wrecked and today the centre pieces are extremely rare; the rings may be classed as 'very rare'.

At the beginning of the nineteenth century, when Canada was expanding rapidly, towns such as Quebec, Halifax, and Montreal felt the need for some form of currency and to this end a series of tokens struck in England were imported to fill the need. Many varieties of these exist, a large proportion of them bear the bust of Wellington on one side and some device (usually the seated figure of Britannia) on the other; some others bear an Irish harp on the obverse, and the legend SHIPS/COLONIES/&/COMMERCE on the reverse. One interesting piece that has definite ties with Canada is that bearing a figure of Hibernia seated holding a harp, the date 1781 below and the legend NORTH AMERICAN TOKEN; the reverse depicts a ship in full sail with the word COMMERCE above. These tokens were circulated in large numbers in North America and Canada generally, having been imported from Ireland, presumably at a much later date than that given on the token.

Following the importation of the tokens into Canada local banks and companies began to issue their own pieces. Perhaps the most interesting of these is that issued by the North West Company in 1820. This company was founded in Montreal in 1784 and operated in an area to the south of the Hudson Bay and as far west as the Pacific coast. The token, which was current for one beaver pelt, depicts on the obverse a beaver resting on a tree stump with the legend NORTH WEST COMPANY and on the reverse a laureate bust facing right with TOKEN 1820 around it. The Hudson's Bay Company also issued tokens about the year 1857. Four types were struck and were current for one, half, quarter, or one-eighth of a made beaver skin, the latter being the unit of currency in the company's forts.

Among the tokens that were struck in Canada, those issued by the Bank of Montreal are perhaps the commonest. In 1835 when many of the tokens that were either lightweight or made of brass were declared illegal, the Bank of Montreal issued a copper token bearing a bouquet of flowers on one side and the value UN SOUS within a wreath on the other. Two years later, during a rebellion by the French Canadians against the government, who they felt did not represent them, an extensive series of tokens was issued imitating those of the Bank of Montreal. They are very similar in design (PLATE XII, 1) and upwards of forty different varieties are known. In 1838 and 1839 the bank issued a number of pennies and halfpennies depicting a view of the side and front of the bank building. The manager did not like the design, however, and most of them were withdrawn, causing them to be among the rarest and most popular tokens in the Canadian series. In 1842 the bank issued another series of tokens, this time showing only the front of the building and these were soon circulating in large quantities (PLATE XII, 3).

In 1841, the colonies of Upper and Lower Canada joined together to form the Province of Canada which in 1858 adopted the decimal currency, striking as its first coins copper one cent and silver five- ten- and twenty-cent pieces (PLATE XII, 4). Nova Scotia and New Brunswick likewise adopted the decimal currency in 1860. The former issued cents and half cents in 1861 and 1864. New Brunswick had a more extensive series consisting of silver five-, ten- and twenty-cent pieces and copper cents and half cents. Of this series, the half cent is the rarest denomination, the reason for this being a rather unusual one. In 1861 cents and half cents were struck at the Royal Mint in London and shipped out to New Brunswick. On their arrival it was discovered that the half cents had never been ordered and they were consequently returned to the mint where, owing to their similarity to those struck for Nova Scotia, a few became mixed in with these coins and returned to Canada where they circulated, thus providing the Canadian series with quite a rare little coin.

Prince Edward Island, which gained its name in 1800 from Prince Edward, duke of Kent, did not adopt the decimal currency until 1871 and then only issued one denomination—the cent. It is interesting to note that throughout the whole of the Canadian series, it is the only coin to have the queen's title in English—VICTORIA QUEEN and that although it was struck at Heaton's mint in Birmingham it does not bear the customary H to denote this.

Nova Scotia, New Brunswick and the Province of Canada united in 1867 to form the Dominion of Canada, Prince Edward Island joining them in 1873. The first coins to be struck by the new dominion were the five-, ten-, twenty-five- and fifty-cent pieces dated 1870. The design for each denomination is basically the same; the young head of Victoria facing left with VICTORIA DEI GRATIA REGINA CANADA on the obverse and on the reverse the value with the date below it, encircled by a laurel wreath with a crown at the top separating the ends of the wreath. On the twenty-five and fifty-cents the queen wears a coronet. Various changes were made in the design of this coin throughout the years. The usual reverse design of the ten-cents was replaced in 1937 by a ship, that of the twenty-five cents by a caribou head and the fifty cents by the royal coat of arms. The five-cents underwent more changes; in 1921 the size of the coin was increased and it was made of nickel instead of silver, the reverse type also being changed. Nickel became a scarce commodity in 1942 owing to its importance in the war effort and for the next two years the coin was made of tombac (88 per cent copper and 12 per cent zinc). In 1944, this time due to the scarcity of copper, the composition was changed to chromium plated steel but the year 1946 saw the reversion to nickel, the original metal. In 1937 when the reverse designs were changed on the other denominations, that of the five-cents was also altered, the value in figures and words above two maple leaves being replaced by a beaver resting upon a log. This design was again altered in 1943; a large V behind a torch, the date either side with two maple leaves below; above and below this central design the words CANADA—CENTS. This design, emblematic of victory and sacrifice is surrounded by a legend on the border in morse code, 'We win when we work willingly'. From 1942 the five-cents was struck as a twelve-sided coin instead of a round one. From 1951 to date the reverse design has again been that of the beaver first used in 1937 but in 1951 a special five-cent piece was issued to commemorate the two hundredth anniversary of the isolation of nickel by a Swedish chemist. The design is that of a metal refinery with the word CANADA above and NICKEL 1751–1951 (PLATE XII, 7). The 1951 type that reverted to the beaver design was struck in steel, again due to a shortage of nickel. This predicament lasted until 1955 when nickel was again used.

The first cent for the dominion was not struck until 1876 and although two changes were made to its reverse design, the principal alteration was to its size, which was greatly reduced in 1920.

The remaining silver coin to be mentioned is the dollar, which was first struck in 1935 to commemorate the twenty-fifth anniversary of the accession of George V. The dies were prepared in London and shipped to the Ottawa mint where these and all subsequent dollars have been struck. The reverse design for this coin depicts an Indian and a trapper in a canoe against a background of the Northern Lights behind a tree. This design has remained constant with three exceptions; in 1939 to commemorate the visit of their Majesties King George VI and Queen Elizabeth, in 1949 to commemorate the entry of Newfoundland into the confederation of the Dominion of Canada and in 1958 to commemorate the centenary of the establishment of British Columbia as a crown colony.

The rapid growth of the dominion made it necessary for her to have her own mint and in 1901 it was agreed that a mint should be set up in Ottawa as a branch of the Royal Mint in London. Construction of the buildings began in 1905 and three years later the first coins were struck, the mint being formally opened by the governor-general, Earl Grey. British sovereigns were struck at Ottawa until 1919 (with the exception of 1912 and 1915) and can be distinguished by the letter c that appears on the ground line just below the horse and above the date. Gold five- and ten-dollar pieces were also struck in 1912, 1913 and 1914 (PLATE XII, 6).

Early in the eighteenth century Newfoundland was separated from Nova Scotia and became a separate province with its own governor. In 1865 the province issued its first decimal coins: the copper cent, the silver five-, ten-, and twenty-cents and the gold two dollars (PLATE XII, 8); no further coins were struck until 1870 when the fifty-cents made its appearance. The cent was not struck again until 1872 and in 1938 was reduced to a smaller size, the reverse design also being changed. The reverse design for the silver and gold coins remained constant with only minor alterations throughout the whole of the eighty-two years of Newfoundland's own decimal currency. As seen above, the province joined the Confederation in 1949 when the dollar depicting John Cabot's ship, the *Matthew*, was issued.

Throughout the entire Canadian series of decimal coinage many coins were struck at Heaton's mint in Birmingham and consequently bear the H mint mark; those struck at the Royal Mint have no mark whilst certain issues struck at the Ottawa mint such as the sovereign produced for England and certain issues since 1917 for Newfoundland, bear the C mint mark. All coins of Nova Scotia and New Brunswick were struck at the Royal Mint, London.

CHAPTER THIRTEEN

Central and South America

IT would be impossible to give more than a very general picture of Central and South American numismatics in this present work. However, to understand fully the evolution of the coinage of the various countries, it is necessary to go back to the fifteenth century when Columbus made his first voyage in 1492 and sighted the Bahamas. In all, Columbus made four voyages, in 1492, 1493, 1498 and 1503, and at the time of his death in 1506 the West Indian archipelago, the east coast of what is now Honduras, Nicaragua, Costa Rica and portions of Venezuela and Brazil had been discovered.

Vasco Nunez de Balboa reached the Pacific coast in 1513 and six years later established Panama city; it was here that the foundations of the kingdom of New Spain were laid and whence all the gold-hunting expeditions set out, north to Mexico and south to Peru. The conquest of the Aztecs in Mexico during 1519-20 and the murder of Montezuma by Cortes in 1521 strengthened the Spanish rule and when, twelve years later, Francisco Pizarro successfully fought his way to Cuzco, the capital of the Inca Empire (having murdered Atahualpa), virtually all resistance to the Spaniards ceased.

Prior to the Spanish invasion, no coins as we know them were used. The Aztecs, a society based on bloodshed with human sacrifice, maintained an accurate system of accounts and each and every person was liable for tax, no matter how young or old or infirm they may have been. This tax was levied according to each person's ability to work and practically any article was acceptable as payment for this debt. Perhaps, however, the item that was most generally acceptable was the cacao bean and Fernandez de Oviedo in his *Historia Eclesiastica de Nuestro Tiempos*, written in 1611, states that, 'There is nothing among the natives that cannot be bought or sold with or for these nuts, just as among Christians with gold doubloons or double ducats. Thus a rabbit could be procured for ten cacao beans; two zapotes (the apple-shaped fruit of the Achras sapota tree) were worth one cacao bean; a slave could be purchased for one hundred cacao beans and a concubine could be engaged for eight or ten beans.'

With such a high value placed on these beans, it is not surprising that some natives became experts in forging them by means of removing the kernel without damaging the skin too much and filling it with earth, thus restoring the nut to its original weight.

In addition to the cacao bean other forms of currency were in use prior and immediately following the Spanish conquest. Pieces of woven cotton called *Patolcuachtli*; grains of gold or gold dust enclosed in duck quills which enabled the amount enclosed to be seen; copper blades in the shape of knives or similar to the tool used today for trimming the edges of lawns; small circular pieces of tin; stone beads, red shells and small gold ornaments in the shape of animals or eagles—all were in use at this time. The pieces of tin are mentioned by Cortes in a letter to Charles V of Spain but unfortunately nothing else is known of them as this is the only reference to them that has so far come to light.

Until 28 January 1527, cacao beans were counted for the purposes of exchange but following a new ruling on that date and until 24 October 1536, the exchange was effected by measure, the size of the measure depending on the municipality where the exchange took place. Following orders issued in New Spain on 17 June 1555, a hundred and forty beans were to equal one Spanish *real*, but by 1636 the price of cacao beans had risen rather alarmingly and the City Council of Mexico City was forced to put a fixed value on them so that they could continue to circulate as coins. The cacao bean remained a monetary unit in New Spain until the beginning of the nineteenth century.[1]

Following the conquest of the Aztecs some convenient form of coinage became necessary; the Spanish had circulated a quantity of coins of relatively high denominations and to alleviate the shortage of small change, private traders in or about the year 1522, caused gold dust to be melted and struck into small discs. These pieces were only marked with the weight and because of the ease with which they could be forged—the gold being debased by the addition of copper—the issue soon became known as *tepuzque*, the native name for copper. Later, in 1526, these pieces were re-melted and struck with the royal coat of arms and

[1] Pradeau, *Numismatic History of Mexico.*

the legend PLUS ULTRA together with the weight and fineness of each coin.

On 11 May 1535 a royal decree was issued in the name of Charles V, establishing a mint at Mexico City with orders of strike silver coins in denominations of three, two, one and half reales. Copper coins were also authorized in the same decree, but it was left to the discretion of the viceroy and the local authorities as to the date of issue.

Both silver and copper coins were struck in 1536, but there is definite documentary evidence to prove that the first coins to be struck at the mint and indeed on the whole continent were struck in gold at an earlier date from some of the tepuzque; the issue was extremely small and no specimens are known to exist today.

In 1544 a vice-royalty was established in Peru at Pizarro's capital at Ciudad de los Reyes (Lima) for the purpose of exporting the treasure of the ancient Inca empire and in the years that followed, vast quantities of gold and silver were shipped back to Spain in the plate fleets, one-fifth of which (the King's Fifth) was bound to be paid to the royal treasury. It has been estimated by Alexander von Humboldt that up to 1803 the amount of gold and silver exported to Spain was little less than £1,000 million. In 1565 a mint was established at Lima and some years later at Potosi also.

At first there were only two vice-royalties; those of Mexico and Peru, the latter including the whole of Spanish South America with the exception of Venezuela which was governed by the audiencia of Santo Domingo. Towards the end of the eighteenth century further vice-royalties were established for New Granada roughly corresponding to Ecuador and Colombia, and for the Rio de la Plata, corresponding to Argentina, Uruguay, Paraguay and Bolivia.

Portuguese interests in the continent were large. During the fifteenth and sixteenth centuries Portugal was the leader of the new era of exploration, such men as Prince Henry the Navigator, Diaz and Vasco da Gama playing an important part in the discovery of the New World. Rivalry between Spain and Portugal in South America necessitated the Treaty of Tordesillas which set up a demarcation line between the colonies of the two countries at 370 leagues west of the Cape Verde Island (a line roughly following the long. 50° west). Brazil, which had been discovered (probably by accident) *circa* 1500 by Cabral had been settled in the coastal regions by private enterprise and in 1532 (PLATE XIII, 4) this area was divided into twelve administrative districts called 'Captaincies'. Later these were abolished and amalgamated into a single executive under a governor general (after 1763 a viceroy).

To the Spaniards it soon became obvious that the placing of too much land and authority in the hands of one man, as had been the case in Brazil, was a dangerous practice and left too many opportunities for independence. Steps were therefore taken to remedy this by subdividing the vice-royalties into governorships and captaincies-general, the viceroy, however, retaining powers of intervention. In 1783 the areas were broken down still further into 'intendancies', eight of these being established in the vice-royalty of Rio de la Plata and seven in that of Peru.

As the area over which the Spanish ruled gradually increased, so more mints were opened, that of Santa Fe de Bogota, in the vice-royalty of Nuevo Reino de Granada, being opened during the reign of Philip IV (1621–65). Further mints were also set up at San Domingo, Guatemala, Santiago de Chile and at Caracas. Many of the coins issued from these mints are commonly known as 'cobs' because of their very crude shape. They are very often practically square and much of the design is usually missing; they are always in poor condition (PLATE XIII, 1). The reason for the peculiar shape seems to be that the blanks were cut by hammer and chisel from a narrow cast bar of silver and if any attempt was made to make them circular, it was by hammering the edges after striking. This type of coin is known to exist of most reigns from Philip II (1555–98) to Charles III (1759–88). The term 'pieces of eight' is a familiar enough expression and although this term can be taken to mean the silver cob eight reales, it is more correct to associate it with the gold eight escudos, also known as a doubloon.

Until the reign of Philip V the gold coins did not bear the portrait of the king, only his name and titles appearing round a coat of arms. Philip, no doubt feeling that his gold coins at least were worthy of his portrait, ordered the type to be changed and subsequently the portrait of the king appeared on the gold coins. It was not until the reign of Charles III that a similar practice was adopted for the silver coins and consequently during this reign coins bearing both the familiar 'Pillars of Hercules' and the bust of the king are to be found.

An interesting anomaly occurred at the beginning of the reign of Charles IV. Ten days after the death of Charles III on 14 December 1788, the Spanish *cortes* issued a royal decree empowering the mint officials in New Spain to continue using the dies of Charles III coins with the addition of another digit to the numeral, thus causing the coins to bear the portrait of Charles III and the title of Charles IIII. Coins of this type were struck in 1789 and 1790 until new dies bearing the correct portrait were cut in Madrid and transported to the mints in New Spain. During this transitional period, some of the dies in New Spain were altered to the correct reading of Charles IV.

Towards the end of the eighteenth century several revolts broke out against the Spanish rule, the general feeling of unrest being accentuated by some of the sons of wealthy Creoles who had been educated in Europe where there was also political unrest.

Knowledge of the recently formed Constitution of the United States of America and the results of the French Revolution helped in causing dissatisfaction with Spanish rule in South America. Champions of the fight for liberty such as Miguel Hidalgo y Costilla in Mexico, Juan Martinez de Rosas and the Carrera brothers in Chile, Narino in New Granada, Monteagudo in Buenos Aires and other more familiar names such as Simon Bolivar and San Martin, each played an important part in the fight for liberty. Napoleon invaded Spain in 1808 and Ferdinand was held prisoner by the French whilst Joseph Napoleon was at the head of the Spanish government. The Spanish-American colonies refused to acknowledge Joseph with the result that no coins or medals were struck for the latter in that continent.

In 1810 a revolution broke out in Mexico led by Hidalgo and Don Jose Maria Morelos y Paron and during the years 1811 to 1814 many coins were issued in the name of Morelos. Since they were produced in whichever part of the country the army happened to be, they were of necessity only very roughly made, usually by casting. The coinage was primarily only a copper one, some specimens in silver are known to exist, but Morelos's authority for the issue of coins, dated 13 July 1811, does not provide for these and some doubts as to their authenticity must therefore be entertained. The usual type for these coins is a roughly formed letter M above the value, i.e. 8.R. (eight reales) within a scroll-like border and on the reverse an arrow strung in a bow above SUD. The eight reales is the denomination most frequently met with, but smaller denominations exist; the four-real pieces that sometimes turn up are forgeries. Some of the coins exist in gold, but as no historical data is available to authenticate them, it is impossible to say exactly when they were coined. Possibly, since the majority of these pieces seem to be of the period, they may have been intended for distribution as gifts among the Morelos supporters, only coined as and when gold was available. Some are no doubt forgeries of a later date.

Following the death of Morelos in 1815 the uprising was crushed and the situation restored more or less to normal although the feeling for independence was still retained. In 1820 there was an uprising in Spain and the situation in Mexico flared up again until General Augustin Iturbide, enjoying again the favour he had lost in 1816 for charging the authorities a percentage for guarding silver trains, formulated a plan for the independence of Mexico under Spanish rule. The authorities were forced to accept these terms and consequently in 1822 Iturbide declared himself emperor and struck coins in his own name. Ten months later he abdicated and Mexico became a republic until the empire of Maximilian which lasted from 1864 to 1867.

In South America the liberation of the continent was due primarily to two generals, Bolivar and San Martin, who in 1816 converged with their armies on the heart of the Spanish-American empire in Peru from the north and south respectively and with the expulsion of the remaining royalists of Charcas by Sucre in 1826, the liberation was complete. In that year, six independent governments were set up; Colombia, Peru, Bolivia, Chile, La Plata and Paraguay and from then on the continent began to fall into the political divisions with which we are familiar today.

With the advent of independence each of the new states issued its own coins based on the decimal system and over the years many of the coins bear the portraits of their country's liberator. In Mexico coins bearing the head of Hidalgo (PLATE XIII, 5) or Morelos, Simon Bolivar on those of Bolivia (PLATE XIII, 2) and San Martin on those of Argentina are examples of this. A very common obverse design for Latin American coins is the head of Liberty and is to be found on both crown-sized and smaller coins.

A wide variety of metals have been used for the coinage. Silver, of course, is a common medium, but nickel, cupro-nickel, copper, bronze and brass are frequently used. Gold is used to a lesser extent and perhaps the commonest gold coin in the whole series is the large Mexican fifty pesos which was first struck in 1921 to commemorate the centenary of Independence. Large quantities of these coins were struck between 1921 and 1931 and from 1943 to 1945, and today these pieces change hands at prices very little in excess of their bullion value.

CHAPTER FOURTEEN

The West Indies

ONE of the most interesting and unusual series of coins resulted from the shortage of currency in the islands of the West Indies in the latter part of the eighteenth and the early nineteenth centuries. It became the practice here to counterstamp coins of various countries to make them legal tender on the islands or, alternatively, to cut them to satisfy the need for small change which in most instances the country owning the island neglected to supply. Owing to the close proximity of these islands to the American continent, it is not surprising that the coin most commonly used for this practice was the eight-real piece, together with its fractions, minted in New Spain, although French and Portuguese coins were also used. The coins were originally brought to the islands by traders or the pirates who were often based in the Caribbean, Jamaica being particularly favoured by the latter.

During the seventeenth century the Spanish dollar of eight reales was generally accepted at 4s 6d, but in some instances it was reckoned at 5s or equal to one English crown. The dollars were divided into fractions, the denominations of which varied from island to island, this being due to the fact that each island's accounts were kept in the currency of the country to which it belonged; Britain, France, Spain or Holland. Usually, the real or 'bit' as it was known, was worth between $7\frac{1}{2}d$ and 9d, but in some cases it was worth very much less than this, there sometimes being as many as thirteen bits to one dollar.

There is no space here to detail all the various types of cut and counterstamped pieces that have been issued, but PLATE XIV illustrates a selection of some of the most interesting. Foremost amongst them are the coins counterstamped for Jamaica (Nos. 1 and 2) where four different counterstamps were used. No cut coins were necessary on this island as ample supplies of small change were available from Britain.

Martinique was originally a French possession, but during the English occupation commencing in 1797 the dollar (No. 3) and its fractions were pierced with a heart-shaped hole, both the resultant 'ring' and 'plug' being passed as currency. Nos. 4 and

8 illustrate both a ring and a plug used in circulation, in this case for Guadeloupe, the ring being current for five livres and the plug for twenty sous.

The island of St Lucia where the French system of accounting was also used is interesting in that no ring dollars were made here, all coins being cut and then counterstamped, see Nos. 6 and 9.

Some of the commonest of the counterstamped coins are those that were produced for use in Tortola in the Leeward Island group, sometimes known as 'the Saints'. No. 5 shows an example of a dollar of Charles IV cut in half and stamped TIATILLA together with the letter 's' repeated three times.

CHAPTER FIFTEEN

Africa

North Africa and the Near East

It seems probable that coins were brought to the African continent by Greek and Phoenician traders as early as the seventh century B.C. By the sixth century B.C., Greek emigrants had founded the cities of Barce and Cyrene, taking as their badge on their coins the silphium plant which they exported in large quantities. The use to which this popular plant was put was twofold; the juice was used as a drug and as seasoning, whilst the the stalk was eaten as a vegetable.

The death of Alexander the Great led, as we have already seen, to internal dissension in the Greek Empire and Cyrene was absorbed into the Ptolemaic kingdom of Egypt. Ptolemy I, who held the satrapy of Egypt for Philip III and Alexander IV of Macedon, took the title of king in 305 B.C. and began to place his name and portrait on the coinage. Undoubtedly the best known of the Ptolemies, at any rate as far as the layman is concerned, is Cleopatra VII (52–30 B.C.) who was famous for her beauty and personality. There are many portrait coins of Cleopatra, most of which depict her as a rather hard-faced woman; her early coins, however, do show something of her alleged beauty. Following the death of Cleopatra (see page 37) Egypt became a province of the Roman Empire and the personal property of the emperor himself, the official who administered it being directly responsible to the emperor.

The Roman colonization of North Africa extended from Alexandria in the east, through Cyrenaica and the cities of Cyrene, Barce and Euhesperides along the coast to Mauretania Tingitana and the straits of Gibraltar. Mints were set up in convenient cities along the coast, not the least of these being that of Carthage situated near the present-day city of Tunis. Carthage, which as an independent city state had been striking coins since roughly the fifth century B.C., produced a long series of coins, most of which featured in some way or other a horse as the reverse type. In 146 B.C. the city was destroyed by the Romans.

In A.D. 429 the two Roman generals in Africa, Boniface and

Aetius quarrelled and Boniface appealed for help to Gaiseric, king of the Vandals in Spain. Gaiseric immediately responded with the result that the Romans were driven out of Africa. Carthage was the one exception, however, and did not succumb until ten years later. Gaiseric continued using Roman coins during the early years of the occupation and also made imitations of them—none, however, with his name on them. Bronze coins were struck at Carthage after the fall of that city and silver coins bearing the king's name first occur under Gunthamund (A.D. 484–96). The Byzantine emperor Justinian I (A.D. 527–65), through his general Belisarius, finally overthrew the Vandals and captured their king Gelimar in A.D. 533.

The mint of Carthage again comes into prominence under the Byzantine emperors, particularly during the reign of Phocas (610–41). In the last year of this reign the Arabs invaded Egypt and soon the whole of the country was under their yoke; it was not until 698, however, that Carthage finally fell to them.

The Arabs at first struck many coins in imitation of Byzantine types but later, the Omayyad Caliphs, who eventually ruled the whole of North Africa from Egypt to Morocco, instituted a new coinage. Owing to the Muhammadan religion prohibiting the copying of any image from nature, both the obverse and reverse of the coinage is devoted solely to legends.

In A.D. 750 the Omayyads were overthrown by the Abbasids, who founded their capital Baghdad twelve years later. Mention of the Abbasids will also be made in connexion with the Seleucid empire (p. 144). Morocco first overthrew the Abbasids in 788 and twelve years later, Haroun Er-Rashid's governor at Kairuan founded an empire which eventually included Algeria, Tunisia and Tripolis. This empire was destroyed in 908 by the Fatimids, and these areas were again united with Morocco under the Almohades in the latter part of the twelfth century.

Algeria and Tunisia later broke away from the Almohades in the early part of the thirteenth century and founded their own independent dynasties. Tripolis, which had been annexed by the Ayyubid dynasty in Egypt in the twelfth century, was later returned to the kingdom of Tunisia in 1510.

The influence of the Turkish empire greatly increased in North Africa at this period so that by the sixteenth century Algeria, Tunisia and Tripolis were all incorporated into the Ottoman empire. After the annexation, Algeria was governed by an official called a *Dey*, appointed by the Turks, this arrangement lasting until the French conquest in 1830. Tunisia was governed by a *Bey*, also responsible to Constantinople and then to the French after their conquest in 1881: it is now an independent republic. In Morocco, the Almohades were deposed by the Marinids; a successive dynasty, the Sharifs, hold the throne today.

The preceding paragraphs show something of the complex history of North Africa and each of the succeeding dynasties produced large numbers of coins of the typical Muhammadan type with legends both on obverse and reverse. Contrary to Muhammadan law, the representation of a lion appears on a gold coin of Mamluk Baibars (1260–77). Baibars, the most powerful ruler of the Mamluk dynasty who overthrew the Ayyubids in 1250, was known as 'the lion' and for this reason placed this emblem on the coin.

The principal mint of the Turkish empire was, of course, Constantinople, but many coins were struck at other mints including Damascus and Aleppo; today, there are mints in both Constantinople and Ankara. It is still the exception rather than the rule to find portraits on Turkish coins, but in 1934 the head of Kemal Ataturk, founder and first president of the republic, was placed on the silver coinage. A short-lived issue of 1 lira pieces struck in 1940–41 bears the head of Ismet Inonu, a later president of the republic.

Tunis, being a French protectorate, now reckons her currency in *francs*, the values being inscribed on the coins both in Arabic and French. There are no portraits at all on this coinage, the more recent issues of which have, since 1921, been struck in a variety of base metals including aluminium, bronze, nickel-bronze and cupro-nickel. The franc system was also introduced into Morocco in 1929 and again the values appear on the coins in both Arabic and French. In 1960, however, the currency was changed and the unit is now the *dirhem*.

For three centuries, following 1517, Egypt remained a province of the Turkish Empire, governed by a *pasha*. In 1792 Napoleon invaded the country and was ejected by the British in 1801. Subsequently Egypt was administered at different periods by Turkey, France and Britain until it gained independence in 1922.

Whilst Egypt was considered part of the Turkish Empire their coins can be distinguished from those of Turkey by the name MISR (Egypt) in Arabic characters. In 1914 Egypt was declared a British protectorate and Hussein Kamil became sultan, striking coins in his own name in gold, silver, cupro-nickel and bronze. The gold (100 piastres) and silver (20, 10, 5 and 2 piastres) bear the sultan's name in Arabic within a wreath on the obverse and on the reverse the value and date appear both in Arabic and English. Hussein Kamil's successor, Fuad, struck coins both as sultan and, after 1922, as king. The republic that was established in 1953 has struck a variety of coins with various designs, most of the lower denominations bearing the head of a sphynx.

Sudan, at one time ruled by the Turks and after 1899 by an Anglo-Egyptian agreement, is now independent and has its own currency. The system is a decimal one based on milliemes, piastres and Sudanese pounds. The coins are of a pleasing design with the legends and denominations in Arabic on the obverse and on the reverse, a camel with its rider.

Ethiopia

The kingdom of Ethiopia is worthy of special mention in as much as throughout its long history, its rulers have struck an attractive and unusual series of coins. Apart from this, however, it provides us with an excellent example of how numismatics can be of service to the historian, for of the twenty-four Axumite rulers known to us from their coins, only five are recorded in history. About the year A.D. 330 Christianity was introduced into the Axumite kingdom which had been established in the Tigre province of Ethiopia, its capital being at Jeha and later at Axum. The kingdom lasted until approximately 920 and during that time its rulers, beginning with Endybis (A.D. 250–75) struck an interesting series of coins in gold, silver and copper. None of the coins is particularly common and the silver are rarer than the gold. A peculiarity of some of the copper coins is that occasionally part of the design is decorated with gold inlay. An example of this work may also be found in the ancient Chinese series as very few pieces of the so-called 'key money' are decorated in this manner.

The obverse of the coins is usually devoted to a bust of the king with a surrounding legend; on the early coins this is in Greek and after about the sixth century the legend is in Gheez script. The reverse, prior to the introduction of Christianity, often bears a bust of the king similar to that on the obverse. After this time the reverse is usually devoted to a cross around which an inscription is placed. Unfortunately, there is very little contemporary information concerning the Axumite coinage and at the present time, due largely to this and to the variations in weight, the relative values and denominations have not yet been ascertained. The specimen illustrated on PLATE XVI, 4, is a gold coin of king Nezana (*circa* A.D. 540–45).

In recent times the coinage consisted of the silver talari first struck by Menelik II (1889–1913) together with its fractions in silver and copper. At present the coinage is based on the Ethiopian dollar of one hundred cents, coins being struck in the denominations of one to fifty cents, all of a similar design. The uncrowned bust of the emperor, Haile Selassie, is on the obverse and the Lion of Judah with the value below on the reverse; this type is reminiscent of that on the coins of Menelik II.

Colonies and Independent Territories

The history of 'modern' colonization of the African continent by Europeans is very largely bound up with the spirit of adventure and colonization that prevailed in the sixteenth and seventeenth centuries. Originally it was Prince Henry the Navigator of Portugal who, by a series of expeditions in the middle of the fifteenth century, laid the foundations for the white settlements of the West Coast of Africa. By the end of the century, the slave trade was well established on the Guinea coast and various British companies were formed in the sixteenth and seventeenth centuries for the purpose of trade with Africa. The Portuguese had been ousted by the Dutch in the seventeenth century and today only a small portion of the continent may be counted as part of their possessions. The British vied with the Dutch over the trading rights of the country and this was further complicated by the entry of the French on to the scene.

In 1750 the African Company of Merchants was formed in England for the purpose of trade with the African coast and in 1796 the company struck a series of silver coins for use in the Gold Coast. It is doubtful, however, whether they actually circulated for they usually turn up in at least 'extremely fine' condition. This series consisted of the *ackey*, its half and quarter, and the one *takoe* or eighth ackey. On the obverse they bear the crowned GR cypher with the date either side of the crown. The reverse bears the arms of the company and on the larger coins negro supporters are added. The legend reads FREE TRADE TO AFRICA BY ACT OF PARLIAMENT 1750; the takoe does not have this legend. In 1818 the type was altered to bear the head of George III on the obverse with his titles around and the date below; underneath the king's head appears the denomination i.e., ACKEY TRADE (PLATE XVI, 3).

In 1957 the Gold Coast received its independence and in 1960 became the republic of Ghana. The new coinage is unusual in that it is, so far, the only country within the British Commonwealth to place the head of its prime minister on the coinage. Struck at the Royal Mint in London, the coinage consists of a silver ten shillings (a crown-sized coin), cupro-nickel two shillings, shilling, sixpence and threepence, and bronze penny and halfpenny. Gold coins, the size of an English two-pound piece were also struck: they pass current at £5.

In 1791 another company was formed, this time with particular reference to Sierra Leone. The Sierra Leone Company struck a more extensive series of coins than its other African counterpart, the issue in 1791 consisting of a silver dollar, fifty, twenty and ten cents and copper cents and pennies: the ten cents and pennies were again struck in 1796. The designs are similar throughout; the obverse depicts a lion crouching with SIERRA LEONE COMPANY above, below is the word AFRICA. The reverse is devoted to clasped hands heraldically shaded to represent black and white. This presumably makes reference to the fact that the country had that year (1791) sworn allegiance to Britain. Above and below the clasped hands are the denomination and the date respectively.

The Gold Coast, Sierra Leone and Nigeria, together with all the other British possessions west of Lake Chad, were counted under the general heading of British West Africa. In 1907 a coinage in cupro-nickel and aluminium consisting of a penny and tenthpenny was issued for the territory of Nigeria. The final issues of halfpennies for this coinage were made in 1911 and two years later a more general coinage was put into circulation for use over the whole of British West Africa. The issue consisted of silver two shillings, shilling, sixpence and threepence, and cupro-nickel pennies, halfpennies and tenth-pennies. The silver denominations bear the crowned bust of the king facing left, surrounded by his titles and the reverse a palm-tree dividing the date with BRITISH WEST AFRICA above and the value below. These denominations have been issued practically every year since then (the silver denominations now being struck in nickel brass) until the reign of Elizabeth II when the Gold Coast, Sierra Leone and Nigeria received their independence. The new coins for the latter country were, like those for Ghana, struck at the Royal Mint in London and consist of the following denominations and designs: two shillings (groundnuts); shilling (palm-tree); sixpence (cocoa-pods); threepence (cotton flowers); penny and halfpenny (crown and value above central hole).

French West Africa and Equatorial Africa

The coinages of French West and French Equatorial Africa are very similar. The design of the winged head of Liberty is used on the obverse whilst the reverse shows the head of an antelope between foliage together with the value either side of the horns. The only variation between those struck for French West Africa and those struck for Equatorial Africa is the legend; both coinages are struck in aluminium. More recently, in 1958, Equatorial Africa has issued three new coins of a different design. Struck in an alloy of copper and aluminium, the issue consists of five, ten and twenty-five francs. The antelope design is modified to show three animals in the centre with the legend above and below; the reverse is devoted to the value within a wreath.

Belgian Congo

To the west of Lake Tanganyika lies the troubled country of the Belgian Congo which became an independent state of the Congo in 1885 and a Belgian colony in 1908. Between 1887 and 1896 a series of silver and copper coins were issued in the name of Leopold II (1865–1909). The silver denominations consist of the five, two and one francs, and the fifty centimes; these bear the bearded head of the king facing left with his titles around. The reverse is devoted to a crowned coat of arms, either above a wreath or with lion supporters. The copper coins have a central hole and therefore no portrait is possible. The obverse design consists of a number of crowned L's around the hole surrounded by the king's titles whilst the reverse shows a large star, together with the denomination and date. After becoming a colony in 1908 the designs were altered but little, with the exception of a new legend which instead of reading SOUV. DEL'ETAT INDEP. DU CONGO was amended to read BELGIAN CONGO. A variety of new coins were, however, introduced at this time. The highest denomination was the fifty francs which, together with a hexagonal two francs dated 1943 and later issues of 1944–48, depict a large-eared African elephant walking to the left.

British East Africa

British East Africa which consisted of Kenya, Uganda and Tanganyika also incorporated the seaport of Mombasa which, until its entry into the general monetary system for the colony, issued a coinage of its own. This coinage, which was authorized by the British East Africa Company, consisted of the silver *rupee* and its fractions, the half and quarter, and two *annas*; copper *pice* or quarter annas were also issued. In 1897 it was decided to make the rupee as used in British India the basis of the currency and for the next three years copper one pice were issued bearing the legend EAST AFRICA PROTECTORATE and the young head of Queen Victoria. In 1905 further amendments were made to the coinage; the rupee was again taken as the standard but the divisions were to be in cents, the highest denomination of which was to be the fifty cents. Following the First World War, the Indian rupee was discarded in favour of the British coinage as the basis for the currency. The florin was divided into one hundred cents with the result that on the shilling the value is given thus: FIFTY CENTS—ONE SHILLING. Later, in 1921, the shilling became the standard and the legend on the fifty cents therefore reads HALF SHILLING.

Throughout the series the higher denominations in silver and cupro-nickel all bear the portrait of the king, whilst those struck in copper valued at ten cents and below all have a central hole and therefore no portrait. East Africa is counted among those British colonies that struck coins bearing the name of Edward VIII; in this instance valued at ten and five cents.

Rhodesia

Prior to the entry of the Rhodesias into the Central African Federation, a special series of coins had been struck for use in

Southern Rhodesia. These coins, first made in 1932, consisted of the silver half-crown, florin, shilling, sixpence and threepence; pennies and halfpennies struck in cupro-nickel did not appear until 1934. A variety of designs were used for the reverses of the new coinage and include a sable antelope and a rock cave drawing—the Zimbabwe bird. The obverse of all coins (except the pennies and halfpennies which have central holes) bear the crowned head of the monarch.

In 1953 a crown piece was struck in ·900 silver to commemorate the coronation of Elizabeth II and the royal visit. A small medallion in the centre of the reverse bears the head of Cecil Rhodes to commemorate the centenary of his birth.

Further examples of wild life are to be found on the seven new coins of the Central African Federation, which were first struck in 1955. The half-crown takes for its reverse design the arms of the Federation; the florin an eagle in flight with a fish in its talons; the shilling a sable antelope; the sixpence, a leopard; the threepence, a flame lily; the penny, two elephants rampant, and the halfpenny two giraffes.

South Africa

The fact that Prince Henry the Navigator opened up the West Coast of the continent to white traders has already been mentioned and it is also to him that the credit must go for establishing Europeans in South Africa. The Portuguese established a trading post at the Cape of Good Hope, but it was the Dutch who made the first major contribution to extensive settlement of the area when the Dutch East India Company founded a settlement at the Cape.

The English, who had used the Cape as a re-victualling post on their voyage to the Indies, captured the Cape in 1795 and held it until the Peace of Amiens in 1802 when it was returned to the Dutch. In 1806 the colony was again occupied by the English who eventually purchased the Dutch colonies of Guiana and the Cape for £6,000,000. The first half of the nineteenth century was marked by a series of tribal wars and further political unrest caused the Boers to set up a republic in Natal. Further Boer settlements were established in the Transvaal and the Orange River Sovereignty, the former being granted independence in 1852 and the latter becoming the Orange Free State. In the Cape

Colony the governing officials agitated for independence in 1850 and a constitution was granted them three years afterwards.

One of the most outstanding figures of this era was Paul Kruger who was born in 1825 at Colisberg in the Cape Colony and had trekked with his fellow Boers to their new settlements. Later, in the war against Britain in 1881, he distinguished himself to such an extent that he was appointed head of the provisional government. In 1883 he was elected president of the Transvaal or South African Republic and his bust appears upon an extensive series in gold, silver and copper that was first issued in 1892.

Prior to this event, however, a wide variety of coins had been used as currency in the South African colonies, including coins of the Dutch and English East India Companies, Portuguese, Spanish and American coins. In 1874 President Burgers issued a very limited coinage of gold ponds which he had had struck in England and it was not until 1891 that the National Bank of the South African Republic was able to begin work on the construction of a mint within the colony.

The first coins were struck in 1893 but were dated 1892. In order to hasten the issue of the new coins Kruger placed an order for gold ponds, halfponds and silver crowns with the Berlin mint who made an error in the die cutting and gave the ox wagon a pair of shafts instead of a single pole; this was, however, corrected on the remainder of the order.

In 1900 Britain annexed the Transvaal, and British coins later circulated throughout South Africa together with coins of the South African Republic. It was not until 1922 that a coinage act was passed ordering a series of coins to be issued expressly for the Union of South Africa and these were struck the following year at the newly established branch of the Royal Mint at Pretoria. The issue consists of ten denominations, ranging from the sovereign to the farthing and bears the bust of George V on the obverse. The sovereign and half sovereign were only issued for a limited period (the sovereign until 1932 and the half until 1926), but the remaining denominations have been issued every year since then. The crown was added to the coinage in 1947 and, like its fellows, has been struck in every succeeding year.

South Africa has now decimalized her currency, the new system being based on the rand, equal in value to the ten-shilling piece: all denominations bear the bust of Jan van Riebeeck.

German East Africa

During the latter part of the nineteenth and early twentieth centuries, a large number of coins were produced for the German East Africa Company, who had trading interests in the whole of what is now Tanganyika, Ruanda Urundi, and Portuguese Mozambique. These coins, first struck in 1890 bear the helmeted bust of Wilhelm II to left and the arms of the company on the reverse. The highest denomination at this time was the silver two rupees. This, together with its fractions down to the quarter rupee and the copper *pessa*, were replaced in 1904 by another series of coins struck for the territory itself. The most interesting coins in this somewhat large series are the gold fifteen rupees and the copper and brass twenty and five *heller* which were struck at Tabora in 1916 during the First World War. The coins for the colony were usually struck either at the Berlin or the Hamburg mint. It became a British Trust Territory at the end of the First World War.

Somalia: Mozambique: Madagascar

Finally, before turning to the coins of Asia, the coins of three countries remain to be considered; Somalia and Mozambique on the mainland and the island of Madagascar some three hundred miles off the east coast of Africa.

Briefly, dealing with the most northerly first, Somalia is at present under Italian trusteeship and has only a very limited coinage based on the *somalo* which is divided into a hundred *centesimi*. The two silver coins—the somalo and the fifty centisimi —depict a lioness below a crescent above SOMALIA. The reverse is devoted to the value, date and mint name (Rome). The bronze coins consisting of the ten, five and one centisimo have a rather pleasing elephant head above SOMALIA, the reverse being somewhat similar to the silver coins.

Mozambique (Portuguese East Africa) has a more extensive coinage based on the *escudo* of a hundred *centavos*. All the coins are very similar in design, mostly bearing the arms of the colony on the obverse and the value on the reverse; the denominations at present in circulation range from the copper twenty centavos to the silver twenty escudos.

The island of Madagascar is the fifth largest island in the world and has been a French protectorate since 1890. The coinage is, however, a comparatively limited one, most of the currency being in note form. Five denominations are at present in circulation, the one, two and five francs being struck in aluminium whilst the ten and twenty francs are an alloy of aluminium and copper. The obverse designs are reminiscent of those coins struck for French Equatorial and French West Africa: the one and two francs issue of 1948 indeed make use of the same obverse dies. The reverse of the one, two and five francs are a modified version of the antelope design on the other French colonial coins whilst the reverse of the ten and twenty francs has a map of the island within a wreath of growing crops.

CHAPTER SIXTEEN

Asia

India

We have already seen in an earlier chapter how, on the death of Alexander the Great in 323 B.C. his empire was broken up and divided between his generals. The resultant liberation of this part of south-west Asia eventually gave rise to the Seleucid empire and the two kingdoms of Parthia and Bactria, that of Parthia being an area roughly equivalent to the old Persian empire. The excellence of the portraiture on the Parthian coins is a remarkable testimony to the ability of the artists employed; PLATE XV, 3, illustrates a typical example of their work. The Greek kings of Bactria and later of India were eventually driven out and their country overrun by the Kushans: the history of the country then becomes merged with that of the rest of India.

The Seleucid empire under Seleucus I included what is now Iraq with its capital Baghdad, the latter, after the Muhammadan rise to power, becoming an independent caliphate under the Abbasid caliphs. One of the best known of the caliphs is Haroun Er-Rashid (A.D. 786–809) of 'Arabian Nights' fame; the coin illustrated on PLATE XV, 1, is a silver dirhem struck at the town of Shash.

India, during the second century A.D., was divided into several kingdoms, the principal of which was the Kushan empire which was formed about A.D. 120 and extended from China to Persia. In the third century the empire was broken up into smaller states, the principal of which was the Gupta empire. Eventually the Guptas were destroyed in the fifth century by the White Huns (the Ephthalites) their supremacy in India lasting for nearly a century. From this time on, there arose in India, many kingdoms who in turn assumed importance during the succeeding centuries. A catalogue of these is not of importance to this book and we may therefore next turn to the fourteenth century when the Mughals began to infiltrate their way into the provinces. Timur (called in Europe Tamerlane the Great) occupied India in 1399 after his Mongol invaders had crushed all resistance and following his withdrawal the empire was left in a state of some confusion.

Eventually, however, the empire was returned to Mughal rule in 1526 under Babar, a descendant of Tamerlane and Jinghis Khan whose vast empire had extended from the Black Sea to the Pacific.

The long list of Mughal emperors of India provides collectors with an extensive series of coins in gold, silver and copper. The coin illustrated on PLATE XV, 5, is of one of India's more enlightened rulers, Akbar I (1556–1605) struck at the Lahore mint; this silver rupee is unusual in that it is square, most of the rupees of the Mughals being circular. The might of the Mughal emperors increased considerably in succeeding years under the guidance of Akbar's son Jahangir (1605–28) and Shah Jahan (1628–58). The former was responsible for an interesting series of twelve gold coins known as *zodiacal mohurs*, so named because of the various signs of the zodiac that are depicted on them; these coins, together with a similar series of *zodiacal rupees*, are some of the rarest coins in the Indian series.

At this point it would be convenient to retrace our steps some two centuries to 1498 when Vasco da Gama sighted the shores of India on 17 May of that year. From this date British interest in the continent begins and Indian commodities begin to find their way to the European markets by way of Portuguese and Venetian traders. In September 1599 a number of London merchants held a meeting with a view to forming a company for the purpose of trading with India. In the following year a charter was granted to the 'Governors and Company of the Merchants trading unto the East Indies' which entitled them to exclusive trading rights with countries between the Cape of Good Hope and the Straits of Magellan. That same year a series of coins was produced for the company which, it is thought, were intended for the use of those trading in the East Indies. Four denominations only were struck —the *dollar* and its fractions, the half, quarter and eighth. The design is the same for each; on the obverse a crowned English shield dividing the letters E.R. each with a crown above, together with the legend ELIZABETH D:G:ANG:FR:ET.HIB:REGINA. The reverse is devoted to a crowned portcullis and the legend POSVI. DEVM.ADIVTOREM.MEVM. At the beginning of the reverse legend there appears the letter O and this is generally taken to indicate the date of striking (1600). Because of the portcullis design the coins are commonly known as 'portcullis' money although the correct title of the crown is an eight *testernes* or one dollar. The coin illustrated on PLATE XV, 6, is the quarter dollar of the series.

In subsequent years both the Portuguese and Dutch became bitter enemies of the British over trading rights in India, the Portuguese in particular having established trading centres at Diu, Damao, Bassein and Goa on the west coast of India. Coins produced by the Portuguese for circulation in these colonies during the sixteenth and seventeenth centuries were only struck in comparatively small numbers and are now rare—later issues are much commoner. Usually, the earliest issues turn up in rather bad condition with only part of the design on the flan due to their having been held in a pair of tongs whilst being struck.

The portcullis coins circulated little, if at all, in the Indies and it was not until the reign of Charles II that the first coins were produced in India for the East India Company. In 1671 the directors of the company ordered a mint to be established at Bombay and in 1677 this was sanctioned by the crown. The coins so ordered were struck in the following year and were in the form of silver rupees; the legend runs THE RUPEE OF BOMBAIM ... BY AUTHORITY OF CHARLES THE SECOND 1678 (PLATE XV, 4).

At about this time, or perhaps slightly earlier, coins were produced for the East India Company at the Madras mint. There is some confusion as to the exact date of the first strikings but various public records seem to point to a mint being in existence there at least as early as 1661. The unit of currency at the Bombay Presidency was, as we have already seen, the rupee and this system was also retained at the Bengal Presidency. At Madras, however, the company's accounts were reckoned in *pagodas* and fractions, the *fanam, faluce* and *cash*. This system was maintained until 1818 when the rupee was taken for the unit of currency, the relation between the two systems being 1 pagoda equalling $3\frac{1}{2}$ rupees and 1 rupee equalling 12 fanams.

During the reign of William IV a number of patterns bearing the head of the king were produced for the East India Company. In 1835 the first of these coins was struck for circulation; two gold coins were issued, the double mohur and the mohur. They are attractive coins bearing the head of William facing right together with WILLIAM IIII KING 1835. The reverse depicts a lion beneath a palm-tree and EAST INDIA COMPANY ONE MOHUR (or TWO MOHURS). Silver rupees, together with halves and quarters and two-anna pieces were also struck, the obverse being similar to that of the gold coins with the exception of the date which appears on the reverse below a wreath encircling the value. The copper coins of this issue consist of the half and quarter anna, the half pice and one-twelfth anna.

The new coins of the East India Company achieved an almost universal circulation in India, but in 1858 the company ceded all its rights to the Crown and from that date on, the coinage refers only to the Queen. In 1876 Victoria became empress of India and the legend on the obverse of the coins was changed to read VICTORIA EMPRESS instead of VICTORIA QUEEN.

Throughout the succeeding reigns of Edward VII, George V and George VI the coinage remained basically the same. Several innovations were, however, made and include the introduction of a circular one anna with a scalloped edge in 1907, a square two annas in 1918 and a bronze one pice with a centre hole in 1943. Like the coinages of many other countries, silver coins gave way to nickel and in 1946 the rupee was introduced as a nickel coin.

At this point some mention must be made of the sovereign and native states of India, the former during the reign of Victoria depicted her bust and title on the obverse of the coinage whilst the reverse named the denomination and state in both English and Persian. Many of the states—the so-called native states—were granted the right to strike their own coins in gold, silver and copper, often bearing the head of their rulers even though they still owed allegiance to the British crown; they frequently bear the name of the British sovereign in native script. The largest of these states was Hyderabad whose rulers issued an extensive series of coins in all three metals.

In 1947 the Indian empire was divided into the dominions of India and Pakistan who issued their own coins based on the system of the rupee of sixteen annas, twelve pies to the anna and three pies to the pice. Ten years later, on 1 April 1957, India went over to the decimal system for her currency, the rupee being now divided into one hundred *Naya Paisa*.

Ceylon

South-east across the Gulf of Manaar from India lies the island of Ceylon. Many indications of ancient civilizations have been found there, but briefly, it was well known to the Macedonians, and traders during the sixth century A.D. visited it many times. The Portuguese established a trading station at Colombo early in the sixteenth century and just over a hundred years later they were expelled by the Dutch who were in turn driven out by the British in 1795, the Peace of Amiens (1802) confirming the country as a British possession.

Brief mention has already been made of the coins issued by the Portuguese for their possessions on the west coast of India and a somewhat similar series of equal rarity was produced for Ceylon. Silver coins known as *tangas* and *double tangas* were struck; the earliest, under Philip II (1598–1621) bear the crowned shield of Portugal on the obverse and either a TA monogram or grid-iron of St Lawrence on the reverse. They have neither legends nor dates.

During the Dutch occupation a wide variety of coins were struck in gold, silver and copper, but two of these types are sufficiently unusual to be worthy of individual mention. Silver *larins* or in Sinhalese *koku ridi*, meaning hook silver, had first been struck in the Persian town of Lar, whence they derive their name. The Dutch, during their occupation of Ceylon, made use of these Persian larins and bent them before passing them into circulation. 'Hook silver' describes these pieces exactly for in shape they are thin strips of silver wire folded in the middle and then bent so that they somewhat resemble a fish-hook; the inscriptions vary considerably.

The other unusual coins are flat bars of copper varying in

Monogram of the
Dutch United East India Company.

length between approximately three and five inches, depending on their value (either 4½ or 6 stivers), and are stamped at the ends with the value. The 4½ stiver bars were rated at half a larin and are also stamped with the monogram of the United East India Company. Both the larins and copper bars are very rare.

The first coins to be struck during the British occupation were *circa* 1801 when copper coins of 1/12, 1/24, 1/96 and 1/192 rupees were produced. In 1803 the first silver coins were issued and were rated at ninety-six, forty-eight and twenty-four *stivers*. These were struck on a very thick flan and bear on the obverse the value within a beaded circle surrounded by CEYLON GOVERNMENT. The reverse is devoted to an elephant standing left with the date below (PLATE XVI, 2).

During the reign of George III the bust of the king appears on the obverse with the elephant motif retained for the reverse of the coins which are now called *rix dollars* (silver) and stivers (copper).

In succeeding reigns copper half and quarter-farthings were struck for the colony as were also silver three-halfpence.

The year 1870 saw the introduction of the first regular colonial coinage. Copper one, half, and quarter-cents were struck and in 1892 the first silver appeared valued at fifty, twenty-five and ten cents. These denominations are still in current use.

British Colonies in Asia

Apart from the two major Commonwealth countries mentioned above, a number of other areas in Asia have at one time or another come under British rule. For more detailed information on these colonies and, indeed, on British colonies anywhere in the world, the reader is advised to consult some of the more comprehensive works such as those written by J. Atkins or Howard Linecar. Suffice it to say here, that a study of the British Asiatic colonies will be most rewarding, both historically and numismatically and many hours of pleasure may be obtained from studying coins of such places as Sarawak under the white rajahs of the Brooke family, the island of Sultana or Labuan and the Cocos-Keeling islands belonging to the Clunies Ross family.

China

To present even a reasonably comprehensive study of the numismatic history of one of the world's oldest civilizations is a task that is unfortunately not possible in these pages. It has only been found possible to highlight some of the periods and issues to indicate the general evolution of the coinage and it must be said here that the dating of these early Chinese issues is a matter that is still much in doubt. The dates and opinions given here are those of Terrien de Lacouperie in his *Catalogue of Chinese Coins from the 7th century* B.C. *to the 7th century* A.D.

As in other civilizations, the earliest form of trade was conducted by means of barter. Tch'eng, second king of the Tchou dynasty, laid down certain rules in 1032 B.C. decreeing that henceforth metal objects should be exchangeable according to their weight. Many pieces, including those in the form of a hoe, passed as currency at this time. By the seventh century B.C. bronze knives had appeared and began to be inscribed with the name of the city of origin, the production of these continuing until about the second century B.C. The familiar round *cash* coin with the square hole in the centre had its origin in a similar type of coin that began to circulate about 950 B.C., the earliest having no marks of any kind, but later issues bear such inscriptions as 'Tchou Tung' (eastern tchou) and later, under the Han dynasty 'Tcheh peh wu tchu' (value 100 five tchou). The range of bronze cash is enormous and spans many centuries; they were still being produced in the nineteenth century.

It was not until the nineteenth century that gold and silver coins were introduced to China's currency, the latter being mainly only used as proofs, patterns and souvenir pieces. It was in 1889 that the first large quantities of silver coins began to be produced, although some isolated issues of silver had occurred at intervals since 1837.

By 1889 the modern coining presses which had been imported into the country were ready to strike coins, the first issues being from Kwantung province consisting of dollar or crown sized coins and fifty-, twenty-, ten- and five-cent pieces.

Until 1912 China was ruled by a succession of emperors; the two that we are immediately concerned with are Kuang Hsu (1875–1908) and Hsuen Tung (1909–12). During this imperial period the various provinces struck their own coins and almost without exception the designs for all these areas are very similar. The obverse bears four Chinese characters in the centre meaning Valuable Coin (of the) Kuang Hsu (régime). In the centre of this there is the same inscription in Manchu script. The reverse bears the imperial emblem of a flying dragon and around this the name of the province in English, together with the weight, thus: FUNG-TIEN PROVINCE 7 MACE AND 2 CANDAREENS. Half dollars read 3 MACE AND 6 CANDAREENS and so on.

During this period also, a large series of pieces known as *sycee* were issued. These are in the form of bullion silver of varying denominations from a fraction of a tael to one hundred taels; the *tael* weighing approximately 565 grains or 1 oz. 3½ dwt. troy. These were not coins in the true sense of the word, but were bullion used for the settlement of debts as from one bank to another. Two shapes were normally used, the commonest being formed rather like an old fashioned hip-bath; they are cast and often bear some stamp or inscription, perhaps dating the specimen to a certain year in the reign of the emperor.

In 1912 the emperor abdicated in the face of a revolution and a republican government was set up under Dr Sun Yat Sen. Thus the Chinese republic was established; it lasted until 1950 when the Nationalist Government assumed power. During the republican period the coinage continued on the same lines as previously, but the obverse of the coins now depict the busts of Sun Yat Sen, Li Yuan Hung or Yuan Shi Kai as presidents of the republic. The reverse is usually devoted to stating the denomination in some form or other. An interesting anomaly occurred on a dollar of 1932 bearing the bust of Sun Yat Sen, when the reverse design of a junk at sea was altered to include wild geese above and the rising sun in the background. Because of the possible allusion to Japan, the rising sun being its emblem and the geese being possible war planes, only 51,000 coins out of 2,260,000 were put into circulation, the rest being melted up (PLATE XV, 3).

Although the republican government had aimed at a national currency, due to the troubled times this proved to be impossible and many provinces retained their independence regarding the currency and struck their own coins.

Both the Nationalist and Communist governments have issued a series of coins in base metals, the former issuing them from the island of Formosa (they bear a map of the island on the reverse) and the latter from the mainland.

Apart from the regular coinage a large number of so-called 'fantasy' coins abound bearing the portraits of generals or governors of some of the provinces. These were intended primarily for collectors and strictly speaking have no place in the regular series of coins; the designs are, however, often pleasing.

Japan

In many respects the monetary history of Japan is not unlike that of China. Barter played a considerable part in the early history of the country and metal coins are not mentioned in Japanese historical literature until *circa* A.D. 700. This reference is to coins which are supposed to have been issued in the fifth century A.D. No great reliance should be placed on this statement, however, and in all probability the earliest coins struck in Japan date from A.D. 708 following the discovery of large copper deposits in the Musaki province. In the same year the Empress Gemmyo succeeded to the throne and following the practice of naming a new era on these occasions, the name 'Wa-Do' (Japan Copper) was devised. This, of course, makes reference to the copper deposits which were to result in a new wave of prosperity for the country. Over the next two hundred and fifty years copper coins known as *sen* formed the basis for the coinage. There were twelve dynasties lasting from the Wa-Do Kaiho *circa* A.D. 708 until Kengen Taiho *circa* 958. In appearance the coins are similar to the Chinese cash with which we are familiar, the obverse bearing a four-character inscription and the reverse being blank. By and large, copper is the usual medium for the coinage at this period, the more precious metals being somewhat in the nature of 'proofs'.

The Japanese, like the Chinese, pride themselves on the elegance of their calligraphy and it was not an uncommon occurrence for the most famous artists of the time, or even for the emperor himself, to have written the original inscriptions for the coins. By the time of the Kengen Taiho period, however, the coinage had become so degraded that famous men no longer considered it a medium worthy of their art.

During the last years of the Kengen Taiho period, the Wa-Do copper began to run out and some difficulty was experienced in finding another source of supply. This, combined with a wave of Buddhism that was sweeping the country, led to large quantities of coins being melted up for the casting of statues of the Buddha. So critical did the situation become that for the next six hundred years, i.e. until 1587, hardly any coins were minted in the four main islands of Japan. During this period many Chinese and Korean coins circulated as well as gold dust, silver plates and silk. Gold plates cast from dust also date from this period and are known as *obans*, the largest weighing nearly $5\frac{1}{4}$ oz.

For nearly three hundred years prior to the introduction of the modern Japanese coinage in 1868 a variety of metals were used for the coinage. Gold obans, silver *Ichibubans* (valued at a quarter of an oban) and other pieces with equally delightful names were coined (PLATE XVI, 1). Copper coins of varying denominations were also issued, one of those most frequently met with being the Tenpo Tsuho (current treasure of Tenpo). This piece was produced in copper and brass between 1835 and 1870 and is oval in appearance, bearing Japanese characters above and below the square centre hole.

In 1868 the Emperor Mutsuhito succeeded to the throne, the era of the reign (1868–1912) being called 'Meiji'. The entire coinage was revised and a mint established at Osaka which began to strike coins in gold, silver, cupro-nickel and bronze. Silver dollar-sized pieces of one *yen* bearing the denomination and fineness of the metal in English were produced in large numbers, together with fifty (half dollar), twenty and ten *sen* pieces. Yoshihito, who succeeded Mutsuhito in 1912 introduced the bronze five *rin* (value half sen) to the coinage and also made more use of cupro-nickel. Under the present emperor, Hirohito, cupro-nickel has again been used and aluminium too is used for the first time in the Japanese coinage.

CHAPTER SEVENTEEN

Australasia

Australia
The first of Captain Cook's voyages in 1770 marks the beginning of British interest in Australia. The year after Cook's third voyage to Australia in 1773 a penal settlement was founded at Port Jackson, now Sydney, the capital city of New South Wales with a population of nearly two million. Soon after the first convicts arrived, it was felt desirable to encourage free settlers to come to this new country and in consequence a settlement of Freemen was established on the Hawkesbury River in 1802. Other settlements soon sprang up along the coastal region and with the increase in population arose the problem of what to use for money. The answer was, of course, barter and practically any coin that come to the island in trade. In respect of the latter, English, Dutch, Portuguese, Asiatic and Spanish coins were amongst those most generally used. The Spanish eight reales which was current at five shillings appears to have been available in only limited quantities at first. In 1813, however, a consignment of these was received which enabled Governor Macquarie to issue a proclamation ordering that the centres of these pieces should be punched out and that both the resultant 'plug' and 'ring' should circulate, the former for 1*s* 3*d*, and the latter for 5*s*. Thus, the so-called 'Holey Dollar' was created (PLATE XVI, 5). Owing to counterfeiting, an attempt was made to withdraw them in 1822, but in fact it was not until 1829 that they ceased to be current. By that time, the centre plug or 'dump' as it is known, was current for only 1*s* 1*d* and the dollar for 3*s* 3*d*.

At last the English authorities had realized their monetary responsibilities to the new colony and a small quantity of coin was despatched to Sydney. Although this supply alleviated the difficulties somewhat, the amount was still insufficient, but with the issue of paper money in the form of Bank and private promissory notes the situation did become a little easier. As we have already seen in both the British and American series, when there is a shortage of small change, private traders invariably take it upon themselves to produce their own token coinage. Australia was no exception and by 1857 the principal currency was in the form of these private tokens. The majority of them are copper pennies weighing on an average half an ounce each, but a number of halfpennies were struck and in most cases they weigh almost exactly half the pennies. In 1860 large quantities of English pennies and halfpennies were imported into the country and a few years later all private tokens were declared illegal.

The Sydney mint was established as a branch of the Royal Mint in London in 1855. Its primary object, together with the mints of Melbourne (established in 1872) and Perth (1899), was to coin sovereigns and half-sovereigns from the gold that had been discovered in New South Wales and Victoria in 1851. The dies were cut in London and shipped to the colony, the first issue of coins being made in June of that year. The designs for this first issue were by James Wyon. The obverse shows the young head of Victoria similar to that used on the British coinage whilst the reverse, instead of the St George and dragon design, bears the word AUSTRALIA with a crown above within a wreath and SYDNEY MINT ONE SOVEREIGN (or HALF SOVEREIGN) above and below. Subsequently, the St George reverse was used, the mint being denoted by the initial letter (S, P or M) on the ground line below St George. The Sydney mint was closed in 1926 but the mints of Perth and Melbourne still produce coins for Australia.

The production of gold coins did not in any way alleviate the difficulties of small change and until the smaller denominations could be produced in Australia arrangements were made for the Royal Mint in London to supply the necessary coin. Accordingly, orders were placed for 1,000,000 each of florins, shillings and sixpences and 2,000,000 threepences. These coins were dated 1910 and depict the crowned bust of Edward VII on the obverse and the Australian arms with its kangaroo and emu supporters on the reverse. In 1911 the first supplies of copper pence and halfpence arrived from the Royal Mint, together with a further supply of silver—this time bearing the bust of George V.

By 1916 the necessary alterations to machinery were completed and the first silver coins to be produced in Australia were issued; the copper at this time was being struck at the Calcutta mint. In 1919 the Melbourne mint undertook the production both of the silver and the copper.

Throughout the years a variety of mints have produced coins for Australia. During the Second World War some of the denominations were struck at Bombay, Denver and San Francisco and may be identified by a series of mintmarks; a complete list of these will be found in Appendix E at the end of this book.

Only two crown pieces have been struck for the Australian series (1937 and 1938) the latter being the scarcer of the two. On the smaller denominations the designs have remained substantially the same, but four commemorative florins have been produced; in 1927 for the opening of the new Parliament at Canberra; the centenary of Melbourne and Victoria in 1935; the golden jubilee of the Commonwealth in 1951 and the royal visit of Her Majesty Queen Elizabeth in 1954.

New Zealand

As we have already seen, it was Captain Cook who made the first contribution to Anglo-Australian history and it was also Cook who opened the way for trading with the Maori natives of New Zealand. On his second voyage in 1772 Cook presented a number of medals to the Maori chiefs as a token of friendship. Apart from a succession of wars with the white settlers between 1843 and 1870 over land ownership, the Maoris have remained friendly disposed towards Europeans until today they are essential and highly regarded members of the community.

The system of barter was used extensively in New Zealand and included such commodities as tobacco, agricultural implements, pigs, blankets, muskets, etc. Those white people who had decided to settle on the islands managed to run their finances tolerably well by using both barter and those coins of various nationalities that came to the islands in the natural course of trade, English, Spanish-American, French and Indian coins predominating.

In 1840 the Treaty of Waitangi was concluded between the Maoris and the British by which New Zealand became a British possession. Following the treaty, sterling was officially adopted as the coinage for the islands, but in fact the variety of foreign coins still continued to circulate concurrently with British and it was not until 1933 that coins were produced specially for the colony. Prior to that date, the shortage of coin had become so acute that those private tokens that had been produced in Australia were readily accepted in New Zealand. In 1857 the first tokens were issued by merchants in Auckland and Dunedin; traders in other towns quickly followed suit so that in all some 140 varieties are known. It was not until 1897 that these tokens were finally demonetized and until 1933 the colony had to rely on supplies of British coins, the groat (which had last been produced in 1888) being perhaps the commonest coin to be found in circulation.

Unlike Australia, New Zealand does not possess a mint of her own and all coins produced for the colony are struck at the Royal Mint in London. The obverse design for the new coinage commencing in 1933 was by Percy Metcalfe and the reverse by Kruger Gray. The obverse shows the crowned bust of George V facing left with the legend GEORGE V KING EMPEROR whilst the reverse designs consist of the coat of arms of the colony on the halfcrown, the kiwi bird on the florin, a Maori warrior on the shilling, a huia bird on the sixpence and carved patu clubs on the threepence. The penny and halfpenny (there is no farthing in the series) were not struck until 1940. The reverse design for the penny shows a tui bird set against a background of kowhai blossom whilst the reverse of the halfpenny depicts a Maori charm known as a Kei-tiki which was usually worn as a pendant around the neck.

There are three crown pieces in the New Zealand series; the first, struck in 1935 to commemorate the Jubilee of George V shows on the reverse Captain Hobson, the first governor of New Zealand shaking hands with the Maori chief Tamati Waaka Nene, referring to the Treaty of Waitangi. Only 1,128 proofs of these coins were struck, some being sold individually at 7s 6d each, whilst others were included in a proof set with the other denominations. The crown was not struck again until 1949 and was intended to commemorate the proposed visit of George VI. Unfortunately, the king became ill and the trip was cancelled; the crowns were, however, still issued. The third crown was struck in 1953 to commemorate the coronation of Queen Elizabeth II.

Apart from the three pieces mentioned above, the series offers only one other commemorative coin—the half-crown struck in 1940 to commemorate the centenary of the Treaty of Waitangi.

New Guinea

The island of New Guinea situated to the north of Australia is at present divided into two parts, the western part being a Dutch possession whilst the eastern is divided into administrative districts of Papua and New Guinea. The Dutch section of the island uses the coinage of the mother country but has a special issue of its own notes. In 1884 the eastern section was divided between Britain and Germany, the latter producing for its territory a series of coins consisting of gold ten and twenty *marks*, silver five, two, one and half marks and copper ten, two and one *pfennigs*. These were struck in Berlin and bear the denomination and date 1894 (1895 on the gold) within a wreath on the obverse and a bird of paradise on the reverse. The German territory was occupied by Australian forces in September 1914 and in 1920 the Allies entrusted its administration to the Australian government.

The first coins for the territory appeared in 1929, the issue consisting only of pennies and halfpennies. Struck in cupro-nickel, these coins have a centre hole and therefore do not have a portrait. The next issue was made in 1935 when shillings, sixpences and threepences were struck: large quantities of pennies bearing the name of Edward VIII were produced the following year.

Fiji

The Fiji islands, of which there are 322, are situated about eleven hundred miles north of New Zealand and Suva, the capital, today forms an important refuelling base for airliners flying the Pacific. British interest in the islands began in 1874 when Fiji became a colony of the British Empire but it was not until 1934 that a separate coinage for the islands was introduced. This issue consisted of the silver florin, shilling and sixpence, and cupro-nickel penny and halfpenny. The two latter have a centre hole and therefore no bust, but the silver coins bear the bust of George V facing left as on the New Zealand coins whilst the reverse of the florin has the coat of arms of the colony, the shilling a native boat and the sixpence a turtle. Recent alterations to the coinage have been the introduction of the twelve-sided threepence in 1947 and the striking of the penny and halfpenny in brass in 1942 and 1943. These latter, together with other denominations dated 1942 and 1943 were struck at San Francisco and Denver due to war-time difficulties; otherwise the coins for the colony are struck at the Royal Mint in London.

Pennies bearing the name of Edward VIII and dated 1936 were produced for Fiji and are not at all rare; they bear no portrait.

Appendix A

NUMISMATIC TERMS AND ABBREVIATIONS

Æ	aes (copper or bronze)
AR	argentum (silver)
AV	aurum (gold)
Billon	a base metal, particularly an alloy of silver with a high copper content.
cmk.	countermark.
Conj.	conjoined
diad.	diademed
Flan	the piece of metal used for the coin
hd.	head
l.	left
laur.	laureate
Ligate	joined together
Mgr.Mon.	monogram
mm.	mintmark or initial mark used to indicate the mint or period of issue.
Obv.	obverse. The side that bears the most important design
Patina	an attractive encrustation brought about by chemical action
Pattern	a coin of a new design that was not adopted
Piedfort	a coin of greater thickness than usual
Proof	a coin struck for presentation purposes and sold to collectors; usually struck from very highly polished dies
Quadripartite	divided into four parts
r.	right
rad.	radiate
Rev. or R_x.	reverse. The opposite to Obverse
std.	seated
stdg.	standing

Appendix B

A CHRONOLOGICAL LIST OF THE RULERS OF BRITAIN AND ARCHBISHOPS OF YORK AND CANTERBURY WHO ISSUED COINS

KINGS OF NORTHUMBRIA
Ecgfrith 670–85
Aldfrith 685–705
Eadberht 737–58
Aethelwald Moll 759–65
Alchred 765–74
Aethelred I 774–9
Aelfwald I 779–89
Aethelred I (2nd reign) 789–96
Eadwulf 796–806
Aelfwald II 806–08
Eadwulf (rest.) 808
Eanred 808–41
Aethelred II 841–9
Redwulf 844
Osberht 849–67
Aella 867

KINGS OF MERCIA
Offa 757–96
Coenwulf 796–821
Ceolwulf I 821–3
Beornwulf 823–5
Ludican 825–8
Wiglaf 828–39
Berhtwulf 839–52
Burgred 852–74
Ceolwulf II 874–7

ARCHBISHOPS OF YORK
Ecgberht 734–66
Eanbald 796–808
Wigmund 837–54
Wulfhere 854–900

KINGS OF KENT
Aethelberht II 748–62
Heaberht ?–765
Ecgberht ?–765
Eadberht Praen 796–8
Eadwald 798–801
Cuthred 801–7
Baldred 807–25

KINGS OF EAST ANGLIA
Aethelstan I 825–40
Aethelweard 840–65
Edmund 865–70
St Edmund 870–905
Aethelstan II 878–90
Oswald (dates unknown)

VIKING INVADERS
Halfdene 872–7
Cnut died 894
Siefred 894–8
Earl Sihtric (dates unknown)
Alfwald 901–5?
Regnald 919–21
Sihtric 921–6
Anlaf Quaran 926–52
Regnald, son of Guthfrith 942–4?
Eric 948 and 952–4

ARCHBISHOPS OF CANTERBURY
Jaenberht 765–92
Aethelheard 793–805
Wulfred 805–33
Ceolnoth 833–70
Aethelred 870–89
Plegmund 890–914

KINGS OF WESSEX/ALL ENGLAND
Beorhtric 786–802
Ecgberht 802–39
Aethelwulf 839–58
Aethelberht 858–66

APPENDIX B

Aethelred I 866–71
Alfred 871–99
Edward the Elder 899–925
Aethelstan 925–39
Howel Dda died 948
Edmund 939–46
Edred 946–55
Edwig 955–9
Edgar 959–75
Edward the Martyr 975–9
Aethelred II 979–1016
Cnut 1016–35
Harold 1035–40
Harthacnut 1040–2
Edward the Confessor 1042–66
Harold II 6 Jan.–14 Oct. 1066

RULERS OF ENGLAND
William I 1066–87
William II 1087–1100
Henry I 1100–35
Stephen 1135–54
Henry II 1154–89
Richard I 1189–99
John 1199–1216
Henry III 1216–72
Edward I 1272–1307
Edward II 1307–27
Edward III 1327–77
Richard II 1377–99
Henry IV 1399–1413
Henry V 1413–22
Henry VI 1422–61
Edward IV 1461–70
Henry VI (rest). 1470–71
Edward IV 2nd reign 1471–83
Edward V 9 Apr.–25 June 1483
Richard III 1483–85
Henry VII 1485–1509
Henry VIII 1509–47
Edward VI 1547–53
Mary 1553–54
Philip and Mary 1554–58
Elizabeth I 1558–1603
James I 1603–25
Charles I 1625–49
The Commonwealth 1649–60
Charles II 1660–85
James II 1685–88
William and Mary 1688–94
William III 1694–1702
Anne 1702–14
George I 1714–27
George II 1727–60
George III 1760–1820
George IV 1820–30
William IV 1830–37
Victoria 1837–1901
Edward VII 1901–10
George V 1910–36
Edward VIII 20 Jan.–11 Dec.1936
George VI 1936–52
Elizabeth II Acc. 1952

RULERS OF SCOTLAND
David I 1124–53
Henry, Earl of Northumberland, 1139–52
Malcolm IV 1153–65
William the Lion 1165–1214
Alexander II 1214–49
Alexander III 1249–86
John Baliol 1292–96
Robert Bruce 1306–29
David II 1329–71
Robert II 1371–90
Robert III 1390–1406
James I 1406–37
James II 1437–60
James III 1460–88
James IV 1488–1513
James V 1513–42
Mary 1542–67
James VI 1567–1625
Charles I 1625–49
Charles II 1660–85
James VII 1685–89
William and Mary 1689–94
William II 1694–1702
Anne 1702–14

Appendix C

LATIN LEGENDS USED ON ENGLISH COINS

A DOMINO FACTVM EST ISTVD ET EST MIRABILE IN OCVLIS NOSTRIS – 'This is the Lord's doing and it is marvellous in our eyes' – *Psalm* cxviii, 23.

AMOR POPVLI PRAESIDIVM REGIS – 'The love of the people is the king's protection'.

BELLO ET PACE – 'In war and peace'.

CIVITAS EBORACI – 'City of York'.

CAROLI FORTVNA RESVRGAM – 'I, the Fortune of Charles, shall rise again'.

CHRISTO AVSPICE REGNO – 'I reign under the auspices of Christ'.

CAROLVS A CAROLO – 'Charles son of Charles'.

CVLTORES SUI DEVS PROTEGIT – 'God protects His worshippers'.

CIVIVM INDVSTRIA FLORET CIVITAS – 'By the industry of its people the State flourishes'.

DECVS ET TVTAMEN – 'An ornament and a safeguard' – *Virgil. Aen.* v. 262.

DOMINE NE IN FVRORE TVO ARGVAS ME – 'O Lord, rebuke me not in Thine anger' – *Psalm* vi, 1.

DVM SPIRO SPERO – 'Whilst I breathe I hope'.

DEI GRATIA – 'By the Grace of God'.

EXALTABITVR IN GLORIA – 'He shall be exalted in glory' – paraphrase, *Psalm* cxii, 9.

EXVRGAT DEVS DISSIPENTVR INIMICI – 'Let God arise, let His enemies be scattered' – *Psalm* lxviii, 1.

FACIAM EOS IN GENTEM VNAM – 'I will make them one nation' – *Ezekiel* xxxvii, 22.

FLORENT CONCORDIA REGNA – 'May the kingdoms flourish in concord'.

F.D. (FIDEI DEFENSOR) – 'Defender of the Faith'.

HENRICVS RVTILANS ROSA SINE SPINA – 'Henry, the dazzling rose without a thorn'.

HENRICVS ROSAS REGNA IACOBVS – 'Henry (united) the roses, James the realms'.

HANC DEVS DEDIT – 'This God hath given'.

HAS NISI PERITVRVS MIHI ADIMAT NEMO – 'Let no-one remove these (letters) from me under penalty of death'.

INIMICOS EIVS INDVAM CONFVSIONE – 'His enemies will I clothe with shame' – *Psalm* cxxxii, 19.

APPENDIX C

IHC AVTEM TRANSIENS PER MEDIVM ILLORVM IBAT – 'But Jesus passing through the midst of them, went His way' – *Luke* iv, 30.

IVSTITIA THRONVM FIRMAT – 'Justice strengthens the throne'.

LVCERNA PEDIBVS MEIS VERBVM TVVM – 'The word is a lamp unto my feet' – *Psalms* cxix, 105.

NVMMORVM FAMVLVS – 'The servant of the coinage'.

O CRVX AVE SPES VNICA – 'Hail! O Cross, our only hope' – *hymn Vexilla Regis*.

OBS(essum) CARL(eolium) – 'Carlisle besieged'.

PAX MISSA PER ORBEM – 'Peace throughout the world'.

PAX QVÆRITVR BELLO – 'Peace is sought by war'.

PER CRVCEM TVAM SALVA NOS CHRISTE REDEMPTOR – 'By Thy cross, save us, O Christ, our Redeemer'.

POST MORTEM PATRIS PRO FILIO – 'For the son after the death of the father'.

POSVI DEVM ADIVTOREM MEVM – 'I have made God my Helper' – compiled from *Psalm* liv, 4.

POSVI MVS DEVM ADIVTOREM NOSTRVM – 'We have made God our Helper'.

PROTECTOR LITERIS LITERÆ NVMMIS CORONA ET SALVS – 'A protection for the letters; the letters are a garland and a safeguard' (to the coinage).

QVAE DEVS CONIVNXIT NEMO SEPARET – 'What God hath joined together, let not man put asunder' – *Matthew* xix, 6.

QVATTVOR MARIA VINDICO – 'I claim the four seas'.

REDDE CVIQVE QVOD SVVM EST – 'Render to each that which is his own'.

REL:PROT:LEG:ANG:LIB:PAR (RELIGIO PROTESTANTIVM LEGES ANGLIÆ LIBERTAS PARLIAMENTI) – 'The religion of the Protestants, the laws of England, the liberty of Parliament'.

SCVTVM FIDEI PROTEGET EVM – 'The shield of faith shall protect him'.

TALI DICATA SIGNO MENS FLUCTVARI NEQVIT – 'Consecrated by such a sign the mind cannot waver' – from a fourth century hymn by Prudentius.

TIMOR DOMINI FONS VITÆ – 'Fear of the Lord is the Fountain of Life' – *Proverbs* xiv, 27.

TVEATVR VNITA DEVS – 'May God protect the united'.

VILL NOV CASTRI – 'Town of Newcastle'.

VERITAS TEMPORIS FILIA – 'Truth is the daughter of Time'.

Appendix D

LATIN LEGENDS AND ABBREVIATIONS THAT ARE MOST FREQUENTLY ENCOUNTERED

A DEO ET CAESARE – 'From God and Emperor'.

AR(CHI) DVX AVS(TRIAE) BG(BURGVNDIAE, COM(ES) FLA(NDRIAE) – 'Archduke of Austria and Burgundy, Count of Flanders'.

ARCH(IDVX) AVST(RIAE) DVX BVRG(VNDIAE) LOTH(ARINGIAE) BRAB(ANTIAE) COM(ES) FLAN(DRIAE) – 'Archduke of Austria, duke of Burgundy, Lorraine and Brabant, count of Flanders'.

BRVN(SVICENSIS) ET L(VNEBURGENSIS) DVX S(ACRI) R(OMANI) I(MPERII) A(RCHI) TH(ESAVRARIVS) ET EL(ECTOR) – 'Duke of Brunswick and Lüneburg, Arch-Treasurer and Elector of the Holy Roman Empire'.

CONCORDIA RES PARVAE CRESCVNT – 'Little things grow through concord'.

D(EI) G(RATIA) B(ORVSSORVM) R(EX) S(VPREMVS) SIL(ESIAE) DVX – 'By the grace of God king of Prussia and Supreme Duke of Silesia'.

D(EI) G(RATIA) R(OMANORVM) I(MPERATOR) S(EMPER) A(VGVSTVS) GER(MANIAE) HIE(ROSOLYMORVM) HVN(GARIAE) BOH(EMIAE) REX – 'By the grace of God, emperor of the Romans, ever august, king of Germany, Jerusalem, Hungary and Bohemia'.

D(EI) G(RATIA) SVE(CIAE) REX – 'By the grace of God, king of Sweden'.

DEXTERA DOMINI EXALTAVIT ME – 'The right hand of the Lord has exalted me.'

DIRIGE DOMINE GRESSOS MEOS – 'Direct, O Lord, my steps'.

DOMINE CONSERVA NOS IN PACE – 'Lord, preserve us in peace'.

ET PATET ET FAVET – 'It is evident and favourable'.

FERD(INANDVS) D(EI) G(RATIA) H(VNGARIAE) ET B(OHEMIAE) REG(IVS) PR(INCEPS) A(RCHIDVX) A(VSTRIAE) S(ACRI) R(OMANI) I(MEPRII) PR(INCEPS) EL(ECTOR) SALISB(VRGENSIS) – 'Ferdinand, by the grace of God royal prince of Hungary and Bohemia, Archduke of Austria, Prince of the Holy Roman Empire, Elector of Salzburg'.

F(RATER) D(ON) AN(TONIVS) MANOEL DE VILHENA M(AGNVS) M(AGISTER) – 'Brother Don Antony Manoel de Vilhena Grand Master'.

F(RATER) EMMANVEL DE ROHAN M(AGNVS) M(AGISTER) H(OSPITALIS) S(ANCTI) S(EPVLCRI) – 'Brother Emmanuel de Rohan Grand Master, Hospitaler of the Holy Sepulchre'.

FRID(ERICVS) D(EI) G(RATIA) REX BORVSS(ORVM) EL(ECTOR) BR(ANDENBVRGENSIS) – 'Friedrich, by the grace of God, king of Prussia, Elector of Brandenburg'.

APPENDIX D

HAC NITIMVR HANC TVEMVR – 'With this we strive, this we will defend'.
HIERONYMVS D(EI) G(RATIA) A(RCHI) EP(ISCOPVS) S(ALISBVRGENSIS) A(POSTOLICAE) S(EDIS) L(EGATVS) N(ATVS) G(ERMANIAE) PRIM(AS) – 'Jerome, by the grace of God archbishop of Salzburg, legate of the Apostolic See, born Primate of Germany'.
HISPANIARVM ET IND(IAE) REX – 'King of Spain and the Indies'.
IACOBVS (DEI) G(RATIA) ANG(LIAE) FRAN(CIAE) ET HIB(ERNIAE) REX – 'James, by the grace of God, king of England, Scotland, France and Ireland'.
IN RECTO DECVS – 'There is honour in right'.
IN TE DOMINE SPERAVI – 'In Thee, Lord, have I hoped'.
INDEI IMPERATOR – 'Emperor of India'.
IOS(EPHVS) WENC(ESLAVS) D(EI) G(RATIA) S(ACRI) R(OMANII) I(MPERII) PR(INCEPS) & GVB(ERNATOR) DOM(VS) DE LIECHTENSTEIN OPP(AVIAE) & CARN(OVIAE) DVX COM(ES) RITTB(ERGAE) S(ACRE) C(AESAREAE) M(AIESTATIS CONS(ILIARIVS) INT(IMVS) & CAMPI-MARESCHAL – 'Joseph Wenceslaus, by the grace of God prince of the Holy Roman Empire and ruling lord in Liechtenstein and Jagersdorf count of Ritberg'.
LVMEN AD REVELATIONEM GENTIVM – 'Light and revelation for the people'.
MAG(NVS) ETR(VRIAE) DVX – 'Duke of all Etruria'.
MEDIOLANI DVX – 'Duke of Milan'.
MO(NETA) N(OVA) ARG(ENTIAE) PRO(VINCIAE) CONFOE(DERATIAE) BELG(II) TRAI(ECTVM) – 'New silver money of the Confederated Belgian Provinces and Utrecht'.
MONET(A) NOV(A) ARG(ENTIAE) REG(NI) POL(ONIAE) – 'New silver money of the kingdom of Poland'.
MONETA REIPVBLICAE TIGVRINIAE – 'Money of the republic of Zürich.'
NON SVRREXIT MAJOR – 'None greater has arisen'.
P(ETRVS) LEOPOLDVS D(EI) G(RATIA) P(RINCEPS) R(EGIVS) H(VNGARIAE) ET B(OHEMIAE) A(RCHIDVX) A(VSTRIAE) M(AGNVS) D(VX) ETRVR(IAE) – 'Peter Leopold by the grace of God royal prince of Hungary and Bohemia archduke of Austria, grandduke of Tuscany'.
PHILIP(VS) Z MARIA REX ANG(LIAE) FR(ANCIAE) NEAP(OLEOS) PR(INCEPS) HISP(ANIARVM) – 'Philip and Mary, king and queen of England, France and Naples, prince and princess of Spain'.
PLVS VLTRA – 'More beyond'.
POST TENEBRAS LVX – 'After the darkness, light'.
REX ANGL(IAE) DNS.(DOMINVS) AQ(VITANIAE) – 'King of England, lord of Aquitaine'.
REX SIC(ILIAE) ET HIER(OSOLYMORVM) – 'King of Sicily and Jerusalem'.
SALVM FAC REIPVBLICAM TVAM – 'Your state safe in union'.
SIT NOMEN DOMINI BENEDICTVM – 'Blessed be the name of the Lord'.

Appendix E

MINTMARKS

LATE ROMAN AND EARLY BYZANTINE MINTS AND MINTMARKS. The following list of mintmarks is not exhaustive, but it does give the major varieties for each mint. It should, however, be noted that additional letters and symbols are frequently combined with the basic mintmark, the former normally denoting the *officina* (workshop) at which the coin was struck and the latter, the issue to which it belonged.

At the western mints, the number of the *officina* was usually indicated by a Latin numeral whilst in the east the Greek system was used. At the mint of Rome therefore we find RP (Roma Prima) for the first officina, RS for the second, RT for the third and RQ for the fourth, etc. The equivalent in the Greek system used at Alexandria would be: ALEA for the first, ALEB for the second, ALEΓ for the third and ALEΔ for the fourth officinae.

The symbols used to denote the issue are considerable in number but the following are perhaps those most frequently encountered: dot; star; crescent; dot within crescent; star within crescent; wreath, leaf, branch and Christogram.

Mint	Late Roman Empire	Early Byzantine Empire
LONDINIUM (London)	PLN: PLON: MSL: MLN: MLL. Closed *ca.* A.D. 326	
AMBIANUM (Amiens, France)	AMB. Closed *ca.* A.D. 353	
TREVERI (Trier, Germany)	TR: TRE: SMTR: TROB: TRPS. Closed *ca.* A.D. 430	
LUGDUNUM (Lyons, France)	LG: LVG: LVGD: LVGPS Closed *ca.* A.D. 423	
ARELATE (Arles, France)	AR: ARL: CON: CONST: KON: KONSTAN. Closed *ca.* A.D. 475	
TICINUM (Pavia, Italy)	T. Closed *ca.* A.D. 327	
MEDIOLANUM (Milan, Italy)	MD: MED: MDOB: MDPS. Closed *ca.* A.D. 475	
OSTIA (the port of Rome)	MOST. Closed *ca.* A.D. 312	

APPENDIX E

ROMA	R: SMR: VRB.ROM: RM: ROMA: ROMOB. Closed ca. A.D. 476	Reopened ca. A.D. 552. ROM: Rm: CONOB. Finally closed ca A.D. 775
RAVENNA (Italy)	RV. Closed ca. A.D.475	Reopened ca A.D. 555. RA: RAV: RAVEN: RAVENNA: CONOB. Finally closed ca. A.D. 741
AQUILEIA (nr. Trieste, Italy)	AQ: AQVIL: SMAQ: AQOB: AQPS. Closed ca. A.D. 425	
SISCIA (Sisak, Yugoslavia)	SIS: SISC: SISCPS. Closed ca. A.D. 387	
SIRMIUM (Srenska Mitrovica Yugoslavia)	SIRM: SIROB: SM. Closed ca. A.D. 395	
THESSALONICA (Greece)	TES: TS: SMTS: TESOB: THSOB: THES: THS: COM: COMOB. Closed during the reign of Leo I, A.D. 457–74	Reopened c. A.D. 518. TϵS: θϵC: THESSOB. Finally closed c. A.D. 620
HERACLEA (in Thrace)	H: HT: SMH: HERAC: HERACL. Closed during the reign of Leo I, A.D. 457–74	
CONSTANTINOPOLIS (Istanbul, Turkey)	C: CP: CON: CONS: CONSP: CONOB. This mint operated right up to the reform of the coinage by Anastasius I, c. A.D. 498	From c. A.D. 498. CON: CONOB: CONOS: COB. Finally closed c. A.D. 1448
NICOMEDIA (Turkey)	SMN: NIK: NIC: NICO: MN. Closed during the reign of Leo I, A.D. 457–74	Reopened c. A.D. 498. NI: NIC: NIK: NIKO: NIKOMI: NIKM. Finally closed c. A.D. 627
CYZICUS (Turkey)	SMK: KV:CVZ. Closed during the reign of Leo I, A.D. 457–74	Reopened c. A.D. 518. KY: KYZ. Finally closed c. A.D. 628
ANTIOCHIA (Antioch, Turkey)	AN: ANT: SMAN: ANTOB. Closed during the reign of Leo I, A.D. 457–74	Reopened c. A.D. 498. ANTIX: ANTX: AN: but after A.D. 528 THϵyPO: τHϵyP'. Finally closed c. A.D. 617

APPENDIX E

ALEXANDRIA (Egypt)   ALE: SMAL. Closed during the reign of Leo I, A.D. 457–74   Reopened c. A.D. 538. Αλεξ: ΑλεI. Finally closed c. A.D. 641

CARTHAGO (nr. Tunis, North Africa)   K: KART. Closed c. A.D. 311   Reopened c. A.D. 534. KART: KAR: KRTG: CRTG: KTG: CT: CAR: CONOB: CONOS. Finally closed c. A.D. 698.

MINTMARKS ON GERMAN COINS SINCE 1871

A	Berlin	E	Dresden (until 1887)
B	Hanover (closed 1878)	E	Muldnerhütte (after 1887)
B	Vienna (1938–45)	F	Stuttgart
C	Frankfurt am M. (closed 1879)	G	Karlsruhe
		H	Darmstadt (closed 1882)
D	Munich	J	Hamburg

MINTMARKS ON COINS OF THE NETHERLANDS FROM 1814

Since the formation of the kingdom of the Netherlands in 1814, the principal mint has been that of Utrecht which is still in operation. Brussels was in use until its cessation in 1830 and during the Nazi occupation of the Netherlands coins for circulation there were struck at mints in Germany (see list of German mm). After the war, American mints were made use of. The other symbols such as a sword, halberd or palm-branch to be found on the coins are marks identifying the mintmaster.

Caduceus	Utrecht
B	Brussels
D	Denver
P	Philadelphia
S	San Francisco

MINTMARKS ON FRENCH COINS SINCE 1795

A	Paris	D			Lyons
B	Rouen	Fish			Utrecht
BB	Strasbourg	G			Geneva
C	Castelsarrasin	H			La Rochelle
CC	Genoa	I			Limoges
CL	Genoa	K			Bordeaux
Cornucopia and torch		L			Bayonne
	Paris(1901-30) or Vincennes	M			Toulouse
		MA (monogram)			Marseilles
Cornucopia and wing		Q			Perpignan
	Paris (1931) or Vincennes	R, crowned			Rome
		T			Nantes

APPENDIX E

U	Turin	Zigzag line	Poissy
W	Lille		

MINTMARKS ON SPANISH COINS SINCE 1479

Aqueduct	Segovia	Scallopshell	Corunna
B	Burgos (until 1700)	Shield with vertical shading, crown above	
B	Barcelona (from 1808)		Tarragona
BA	Barcelona	Shield, quartered, with vertical shading and star above M or star above castle	
C, crowned	Cadiz		
C	Cataluna		
C	Cuenca		
C, with A in centre	Cuenca		Palma, Majorca
C	Reus (from 1808)	Star, five pointed	Madrid (since 1895)
CA	Zaragoza		
G	Granada	Star, six pointed	Madrid (since 1833)
GNA	Gerona		
ILD	Lerida	Star, seven pointed	Seville (since 1833)
J	Jubia		
M, crowned	Madrid	Star, eight pointed	Barcelona (since 1833)
M	Madrid		
MD (ligate)	Madrid	T	Toledo
P	Palma, Majorca (1812)	TOR:SA within rectangle	Tortosa
P, PA	Pamplona	V	Valencia
Pomegranate	Granada	Wavy lines (three or four)	Valladolid
S	Seville		

MINTMARKS ON COINS OF THE U.S.A.

C	Charlotte, North Carolina (gold only)	D	Denver, Colorado (after 1906)
CC	Carson City, Nevada	O	New Orleans, Louisiana
D	Dahlonega, Georgia (gold only, 1838–61)	P	Philadelphia, Pennsylvania
		S	San Francisco, California

APPENDIX E

MINTMARKS ON CANADIAN COINS

C Ottawa, Ontario
H Heaton Ltd., Birmingham, England

Coins without a mintmark struck prior to 1908 were struck at the Royal Mint, London.

Coins without a mintmark struck after 1908 were struck at the Ottawa mint.

MINTMARKS ON AUSTRALIAN COINS

A A. Perth
D Denver
H Heaton Ltd. Birmingham
I Calcutta
M Melbourne
PL Royal Mint, London
S San Francisco

Dot before and after PENNY and I on obverse	Bombay
Dot before and after HALFPENNY and I on obverse	Bombay
Dot before and after PENNY	Bombay
Dot after HALFPENNY	Perth
Dot before SHILLING	Perth
Dot above scroll on reverse	Sydney
Dot below scroll on reverse	Melbourne

Coins without mint marks were also struck at:

London from 1910–15
Melbourne from 1921–56
Perth penny 1922
Perth halfpenny 1955
Sydney from 1919–26

APPENDIX E

SPANISH-AMERICAN AND LATIN-AMERICAN MINTMARKS

In some cases coins struck in the Latin American mints bear the actual names of the towns in which they were struck, but in many instances, particularly with regard to the Spanish American mints, no such names are given, the mints being identified by a letter or monogram; these are as follows:

Mark	Mint
A, AS, $\overset{S}{A}$	Alamos, Mexico
B, B	Bogota, Columbia
B	Bahia, Brazil
C	Cuiaba, Brazil
C, CN, CN, $\overset{N}{C}$	Culiacan, Mexico
C, CO, CUZO (mgr.)	Cuzco, Peru
C^E	Real del Catorce, Mexico
CH, CA, CA	Chihuahua, Mexico
CR	San Jose, Costa Rica
D, Do	Durango, Mexico
Eo, Mo	Tlalpam, Mexico
FS	Santa Fe de Bogotá
G	Goias, Brazil
GA	Guadalajara, Mexico
G	Guatemala
GC	Guadelupe y Calvo, Mexico
Go, $\overset{o}{G}$, G	Guanajuato, Mexico
Ho, Ho, $\overset{o}{H}$	Hermosillo, Mexico
L, LM, LR LIMA (mgr.)	Lima, Peru
M	Minaes Geraes, Brazil
M	Mendoza, Argentina
M	Medellin, Columbia
ME	Lima, Peru
M, $\overline{M}$, $\overset{o}{M}$, $\overset{o}{M}$, M^o, Mo, Mxo .M.X. (1732-33)	Mexico City, Mexico
NG	Nuevo (Guatemala), Guatemala
NR, $\overset{oo}{NR}$ (and variants)	(Nuevo Reino) Santa Fe de Bogotá, Columbia
NR	Leon de Nicaragua, Nicaragua
O, OA, Ⓞ, OKA	Oaxaca, Mexico
P	Lima (1568-70), Peru
P	Pernambuco, Brazil
P, PN, P^n	Popayan, Columbia
P, PTS, PTR (mgr. and variants)	Potosi, Bolivia
Pi	San Luis, Potosi, Mexico
R	Rio de Janeiro Brazil
RA	Rioja, Argentina
S, $\overset{o}{S}$	Santiago, Chile
S, SD	San Domingo, Costa Rica
SE	Santiago del Estero, Argentina
SF	Santa Fe de Bogotá
S:L.P.	San Luis Potosi, Mexico
SM	Santa Marta, Columbia
T, TEG	Tegucigalpa, Honduras
TC	Tierra Caliente, Mexico
VA	Valdista, Chile
Z, Zs, ZS	Zacatecas, Mexico

Appendix F

DENOMINATIONS OF THE WORLD

In the following list, only the *denominations* that are at present (March 1961) in circulation are quoted, and in order that it may remain accurate for a greater period, no attempt has been made to indicate the different types that occur for each denomination.

Aden	(see British East Africa)
Afghanistan	25 & 50 puls; 2 & 5 Afghanis
Africa, British East	1, 5, 10 & 50 cents; 1 shilling
Africa, British West	1/10, ½ & 1 penny; 3 & 6 pence; 1 shilling
Africa, French Equatorial	1, 2, 5, 10 & 25 francs
Africa, French West	1, 2, 5, 10 & 25 francs
Africa, South	¼, ½ & 1 penny; 3 & 6 pence; 1, 2, 2½ & 5 shillings; ½, 1, 2½, 5, 10, 20 & 50 cents
Albania	½, 1, 2 & 5 lek
Algeria	20, 50 and 100 francs. Lower denominations, coins of Metropolitan France
America, United States of,	1, 5, 10, 25 & 50 cents; 1 dollar
Angola	50 centavos; 1, 2½, 10 & 20 escudos
Antigua	(see British Caribbean Territories)
Antilles, Netherlands	1, 2½ & 5 cents; 1/10, ¼, 1 & 2½ gulden
Argentina	1, 2, 5, 10, 20 & 50 centavos; 1 peso
Australia	½ & 1 penny; 3 & 6 pence; 1, 2 & 5 shillings
Austria	1, 2, 5, 10 & 50 groschen; 1, 5, 10, 25 & 50 schilling
Barbados	(see British Caribbean Territories)
Bermuda	Crown; British coinage
Belgian Congo	10, 20 & 50 centimes; 1, 2 & 5 francs
Belgium	20, 25 & 50 centimes; 1, 5, 20, 50 & 100 francs
Borneo	(see Malaya)
Brazil	10, 20 & 50 centavos; 1 & 2 cruzeiros
British Caribbean Territories (eastern group)	½, 1, 2, 5, 10, 25 & 50 cents
British Guiana	(see British Caribbean Territories)
Brunei	(see Malaya)

APPENDIX F

Bulgaria	1, 3, 5, 10 & 20 stotinki
Burma	1, 5, 10, 25 & 50 pyas; ¼ & ½ rupee; 1 kyat
Cambodia	10, 20 & 50 sen
Cameroons, French	1, 2, 5, 10, 25 & 50 francs
Canada	1, 5, 10, 25 & 50 cents; 1 dollar
Cape Verde	1, 2½ & 10 escudos
Ceylon	½, 1, 2, 5, 10, 25 & 50 cents; 1 & 5 rupees
Chile	20 centavos; 1 & 10 pesos
China, People's Republic	1, 2 & 5 fen
Colombia	1, 2, 5, 10, 20 & 50 centavos; 1 peso
Costa Rica	5, 10, 25 & 50 centimos; 1 & 2 colones
Cuba	1, 2, 5, 10, 20, 25, 40 & 50 centavos; 1 peso
Curaçao	(see Antilles)
Cyprus	3, 5, 25, 50 & 100 mils
Czechoslovakia	1, 3, 5, 10 & 25 Heller; 1, 10, 25, 50 & 100 crowns
Denmark	1, 2, 5, 10 & 25 øre; 1, 2 & 5 kroner
Dominica	(see British Caribbean Territories)
Dominica, Republic of	1, 5, 10, 25 & 50 centavos; 1 peso
Ecuador	1, 5, 10 & 20 centavos; 1 sucre
Egypt (see also U.A.R.)	1, 5, 10 & 20 milliemes; 5, 10, 20, 25 & 50 piastres
Ethiopia	1, 5, 10, 25 & 50 cents
Falkland Islands	British coinage
Faroe Islands	British coinage
Fiji	½ & 1 penny; 3 & 6 pence; 1 & 2 shillings
Finland	1, 5, 10, 20, 50, 100, 200, 500 & 1,000 markkaa
Formosa	10, 20 & 50 cents
France	1, 2, 5, 10, 20, 50 & 100 francs; 1 & 5 'heavy' new francs (1 NF = 100 old)
Germany, Eastern	1, 5, 10 & 50 pfennig; 1 & 2 Deutsche marks
Germany, Federal Republic	1, 2, 5, 10 & 50 pfennig; 1, 2 & 5 Deutsche marks
Ghana	½ & 1 penny; 3 & 6 pence; 1, 2 & 10 shillings
Gibraltar	British coinage
Great Britain	½ & 1 penny; 3 & 6 pence; 1 & 2 shillings; halfcrown, crown
Greece	5, 10, 20 & 50 lepta; 1, 2, 5, 10 & 20 drachmai
Greenland	25 & 50 øre; 1 5 & 10 kroner
Grenada	(see British Caribbean Territories)
Guadeloupe	French coinage
Guatemala	½, 1, 2, 5, 10 & 25 centavos; ¼ quetzal

Guernsey	1, 2, 4 & 8 doubles; 3 pence
Guiana, French	French coinage
Guinea, Portuguese	50 centavos; 1, 2½, 10 & 20 escudos
Haiti	5, 10, 20 & 50 centimes
Honduras, British	1, 5, 10, 25 & 50 cents
Hong Kong	5, 10 & 50 cents; 1 dollar
Hungary	2, 5, 10, 20 & 50 filler; 1, 2, 5, 10, 20 & 25 forints
Iceland	1 Eyrir; 2, 5, 10 & 25 aurar; 1 & 2 kronur
India	1 pice; 1, 2, 5, 10, 25 & 50 naya paisa; 1 anna; ¼, ½ & 1 rupee
India, Portuguese	Portuguese coinage
Indonesia	1, 5, 10, 25 & 50 sen
Iran	5, 10, 25 & 50 dinars; 1, 2, 5 & 10 rials
Iraq	1, 2, 5, 10, 25, 50, 100 & 200 fils
Ireland, Northern	British coinage
Ireland, Republic of	¼, ½ & 1 penny; 3 & 6 pence; 1, 2 & 2½ shillings
Israel	1, 5, 10, 25, 50, 100 & 250 pruta; 1 & 5 pounds
Italy	1, 2, 5, 10, 20, 50, 100 & 500 lire
Jamaica	¼, ½ & 1 penny, also British coinage
Japan	1, 5, 10, 50 & 100 yen
Jersey	1/24, 1/12 & ¼ shilling
Jordan	1, 5, 10, 20, 50 & 100 fils
Kenya	(see British East Africa)
Korea, Republic of	10, 50 & 100 hwan
Labuan	(see Malaya)
Laos	10, 20 & 50 centimes
Lebanon	1, 2½, 5, 10, 25 & 50 piastres
Liberia	1, 5, 10, 25 & 50 cents
Libya	1, 2 & 5 milliemes; 1 & 2 piastres
Liechtenstein	Swiss coinage
Luxemburg	25 centimes; 1 & 5 francs
Macao	5, 10 & 50 avos; 1 & 5 patacas
Madagascar	1, 2, 5, 10 & 20 francs
Malayan archipelago	1, 5, 10, 20 & 50 cents; 1 dollar
Malta	British coinage
Martinique	French coinage
Mauritius	1, 2, 5 & 10 cents; ¼, ½ & 1 rupee
Mexico	1, 5, 10, 20 & 50 centavos; 1, 5 & 10 pesos
Miquelon	(see St Pierre)
Monaco	1, 2, 5, 10, 20, 50 & 100 francs; 1 & 5 new francs (1 NF = 100 old)
Mongolia	1, 2, 5, 10, 15 & 20 mung

Morocco	1, 2, 5, 10, 20, 50, 100, 200 & 500 francs; 1 dirhem (100 francs)
Mozambique	20 & 50 centavos; 1, 2½, 5, 10 & 20 escudos
Muscat and Oman, Sultanate of	¼ anna; 2, 3, 5, 10, 20 & 50 biazas; ½ & 1 rial
Nepal	1, 2, 4, 5, 10, 20, 25 & 50 pice; 1 rupee
Netherlands	1, 5, 10 & 25 cents; 1 & 2½ gulden
New Caledonia	1 & 2 francs
New Guinea, Netherlands	Dutch coinage
New Zealand	½ & 1 penny; 3 & 6 pence; 1, 2, 2½ & 5 shillings
Nicaragua	1, 5, 10, 25 & 50 centavos
Nigeria	½ & 1 penny; 3 & 6 pence; 1 & 2 shillings
Norway	1, 2, 5, 10, 25 & 50 øre; 1 krone
Oceania, French	(see Tahiti)
Pakistan	1 pie; 1 pice; ½, 1, 2, 4 & 8 annas; ¼, ½ & 1 rupee
Panama	1, 1¼, 2½, 5, 10, 25 & 50 centesimos; 1 balboa
Paraguay	1, 5, 10, 15, 25 & 50 centimos
Peru	1, 2, 5, 10 & 20 centavos; ½ & 1 sol
Philippines	1, 5, 10, 20 & 50 centavos
Poland	1, 2, 5, 10, 20 & 50 groszy; 1 & 2 zlote
Portugal	10, 20 & 50 centavos; 1, 2½, 5 & 10 escudos
Reunion	1, 2, 5, 10 & 20 francs
Rhodesia (Northern and Southern) Nyasaland	½ & 1 penny; 3 & 6 pence; 1, 2, 2½ & 5 shillings
Roumania	1, 3, 5, 10, 25 & 50 bani
Russia	(see U.S.S.R.)
Ruanda Urundi	1 franc
Salvador	25 & 50 centavos
Saudi Arabia	¼, ½, 1, 2 & 4 Qursh; 1 sovereign
Seychelles	1, 2, 5, 10 & 25 cents; ½ & 1 rupee
Singapore	(see Malaya)
Somaliland, British	(see British East Africa)
Somaliland, French	1, 2, 5 & 20 francs
Somaliland, Italian	1, 5, 10 & 50 centisimi; 1 somalo
Spain	10 & 50 centimos; 1, 2½, 5, 25 & 50 pesetas
St Kitts	(see British Caribbean Territories)
St Lucia	(see British Caribbean Territories)
St Pierre and Miquelon	1 & 2 francs
St Thomas and Prince Islands	50 centavos; 1, 2½, 5 & 10 escudos
St Vincent	(see British Caribbean Territories)
Sudan	1, 2, 5 & 10 milliemes; 2, 5 & 10 piastres

APPENDIX F

Surinam	Dutch coinage
Sweden	1, 2, 5, 10, 25 & 50 øre; 1, 2 & 5 kroner
Switzerland	1, 2, 5, 10, 20 & 50 centimes; 1, 2, 5, 25 & 50 francs
Syria (see also U.A.R.)	1 Syrian livre; 1, 2½, 5, 10, 25 & 50 piastres; ½ & 1 gold livre (1 gold livre = 15 Syrian livres
Tahiti	1 & 2 francs
Tanganyika	(see British East Africa)
Thailand	1, 5, 10, 25 & 50 stang
Timor, Portuguese	10, 20 & 50 avos
Tobago	(see British Caribbean Territories)
Togo	5 & 10 francs; 1 & 2 francs as used in French Equatorial Africa
Tonga	British, Australian, Fijian and New Zealand coinage
Trinidad	(see British Caribbean Territories)
Tunisia	½, 1, 2, 5, 20, 50 & 100 francs
Turkey	1, 2½, 5, 10, 25 & 50 kurus; 1 lira
Uganda	(see British East Africa)
United Arab Republic	20 milliemes; 10 piastres
Uruguay	1, 2, 5, 10, 20 & 50 centesimos; 1 peso
U.S.S.R.	1, 2, 3, 5, 10, 15, 20 & 50 copecks; 1 rouble
Vatican city	1, 2, 5, & 10 lire
Venezuela	5, 12½, 25 & 50 centimos; 1, 2 & 5 bolivares
Vietnam	10, 20 & 50 cents
Yemen (see also U.A.R.)	1 Halala; 1 bogash; ½ & 1 ryal
Yugoslavia	50 para; 1, 2, 5, 10, 20 & 50 dinars
Zanzibar	(see British East Africa)

Bibliography

In some instances books that are regarded as standard reference works have been omitted from this list due to their rarity and high price. Special attention has, however, been paid to those books that may be more easily obtained or are still in print.

GENERAL

Atkins, J., *Coins and Tokens of the Possessions and Colonies of the British Empire*. London, 1889.
Friedberg, R., *Gold Coins of the World*, A.D. 600–1958. New York 1958.
Hill, G. F., *Becker the Counterfeiter*, second edn. London 1955.
Linecar, H. W. A., *British Commonwealth Coinage*. London 1959.
Raymond, Wayte, *Coins of the World, Nineteenth Century Issues*. New York, 1953.
Raymond, Wayte, *Coins of the World, Twentieth Century Issues*, fifth edn. New York. 1955.
Thomsen, Christian J., *Description des Monnaies du Moyen-Age*. Copenhagen 1873.
Von Schrötter, Friedrich, *Wörterbuch der Münzkunde*. Berlin. 1930.
Wright, L. V. W., *Colonial and Commonwealth Coins*. London 1959.
Yeoman, R. S., *A Catalogue of Modern World Coins*, third edn. Racine, Wis. 1959.

AFRICA

Mazard, J., *Histoire Monétaire et Numismatique des Colonies et de l'Union Française 1670–1952*. Paris 1953.
Parsons, H. A., *The Colonial Coinages of British Africa*. London 1950.
Schlumberger, G., *Numismatique de l'Orient Latin*, reprint. Graz 1954.

AMERICA

Breton, P. N., *Illustrated History of Coins and Tokens Relating to Canada*. Montreal 1894.
Burzio, Humberto F., *Diccionario de la Moneda Hispano-Americana*. Santiago de Chile 1958.
Calico, X. F., *Aportacion a la Historia Monetaria de Santa Fé de Bogotá*. Barcelona 1953.
Charlton, J. E., 1960 *Standard Catalogue of Canadian Coins, Tokens and Paper Money*. Toronto 1960.

Crosby, Sylvester S., *The Early Coins of America*. Boston 1875.
Guttag, Julius, *Sale Catalogue of the Collection*. New York 1929.
Pradeau, Dr A. F., 'A study of the Coinage of the Mexican Independent Leader Morelos', *The Numismatist Magazine*, August 1947.
Pradeau, Dr A. F., *Numismatic History of Mexico*. Los Angeles 1938.
Prober, K., *Historia Numismatica de Guatemala*. Sao Paulo 1954.
Wood, Howland, 'Cut and Counterstamped Coins of the West Indies', *American Numismatic Society Journal*. New York 1915.
Yeoman, R. S., *A Guide Book of United States Coins*, fourteenth edn. Racine 1960.

ANCIENT

Askew, G., *The Coinage of Roman Britain*. London 1951.
Goodacre, H., *A Handbook of the coinage of the Byzantine Empire*. London 1957.
Grant, M., *Roman History from Coins*. Cambridge 1958.
Jacob, K. A., *Coins and Christianity*. London 1958.
Mattingly, H., *Roman Coins*, second edn. London 1960.
Narain, A. K., *The Indo-Greeks*. Oxford 1957.
Seaby, H. A. and Kozolubski, J., *Greek Coins and their Values*. London 1959.
Seaby, H. A., *Roman Coins and their Values*. London 1954.
Seltman, C., *Greek Coins*. London 1955.
Tarn, W. W., *The Greeks in Bactria and India*. Cambridge 1951.

ASIA

Jacobs, N. and Vermeule, C. C., *Japanese Coinage*. New York 1953.
Kann, E., *Illustrated Catalogue of Chinese Coins*. Hong Kong 1954.
Lacouperie, Terrien de, *Catalogue of Chinese Coins from the Seventh Century B.C. to the Seventh Century A.D.* British Museum Catalogue, London 1892.
Lane-Poole, Stanley, *The Muhammadan dynasties*. Paris 1925.
Prawdin, Michael., *The Mongol Empire*. London 1953.
Scholten, C., *Coins of the Dutch Overseas Territories, 1601–1948*. Amsterdam 1953.
Schroeder, Albert, *Annam, Etudes Numismatiques*. Paris 1905.
Wang, Yü-Ch'üan, *Early Chinese Coinage*. American Numismatic Society publication, New York 1951.

AUSTRALASIA

Andrews, Dr A., *Australasian Tokens and Coins*. Sydney 1921.
Meek, W. F. W., *Currency tokens of New Zealand*. Dunedin 1951.
Sutherland, Allan, *Numismatic History of New Zealand*. Wellington 1941.

BIBLIOGRAPHY

BRITISH

Brooke, G. C., *English Coins*, third edn. London 1955.
Craig, Sir John, *The Mint*. Cambridge 1953.
Grueber, H. A., *Handbook of the Coins of Great Britain and Ireland in the British Museum*. London 1899.
Mack, Commander R. P., *The Coinage of Ancient Britain*. London 1953.
North, J. J., *English Hammered Coinage*. London 1960.
Oman, Sir Charles, *The Coinage of England*. Oxford 1931.
Seaby, H. A., *The English Silver Coinage from 1649*. London 1957.
Seaby, H. A. (Ed.), *Notes on English Silver Coins 1066-1648*. London 1948.
Seaby, H. A., *Standard Catalogue of the Coins of Great Britain and Ireland*. London 1960.
Seaby, P. J., *The Story of the English Coinage*. London 1952.
Stewart, I. H., *The Scottish Coinage*. London 1955.
Rayner, P. A., *The Designers and Engravers of the English Milled Coinage, 1662-1953*. London 1954.
Waters, A. W., *Notes on Eighteenth Century Tokens*. London 1954.
Waters, A. W., *Notes on Nineteenth Century Silver Tokens*, London.1957

EUROPE

Chaudoir, Baron S. de, *Aperçu sur les Monnaies Russes*. St Petersburg 1836.
Coffin, Joseph, *Coins of the Popes*. New York 1946.
Dasi, Tomas, *Estudio de los Reales de A Ocho*. Valencia 1951.
Davenport, John S., *European Crowns, 1700-1800*. Galesburg 1961.
Davenport, John S., *European Crowns since 1800*. Galesburg 1947.
Davenport, John S., *German talers, 1700-1800*. Galesburg 1958.
Davenport, John S., *German talers, since 1800*. Galesburg 1949.
Farres, O. G., *Historia de la Moneda Hispanola*. Madrid 1960.
Gaettens, R., *Inflationen*. Munich 1955.
Glück, H. and Hesselblad, C. G., *Årtalsforteckning över Svenska Mynt med Värderingspriser: Gustaf Vasa-Gustaf VI 1521-1959*. Stockholm, 1959.
Gumowski, Prof. Dr Marian, *Handbuch der Pölnischen Numismatik*, reprint. Graz 1960.
Hazlitt, W. C., *The Coinage of the European Continent*. London 1893.
Heiss, Aloiss, *Descripcion General de las Monedas Hispano-Cristianas*. Madrid 1867.
Hutten-Czapski, Emeric, *Catalogue de la Collection des Médailles et Monnaies Polonaises*, reprint. Graz 1957.
Jaeger, K., *Die Deutschen Reichsmünzen, seit 1871*. Basel 1959.
Mort, S. R., *Coins of the Hapsburg Emperors and Related Issues, 1619-1919*. Melbourne 1959.

Petrov, V. I., *Catalogue des Monnaies Russes*. Moscow 1899.
Prou, Maurice, *Catalogue des Monnaies Mérovingiennes*. Paris 1892.
Prou, Maurice, *Catalogue des Monnaies Carolingiennes*. Paris 1896.
Reis, P. B., *Precario das Moedas Portuguesas:* Vol. I 1140–1640. Lisbon 1956. Vol. II 1640–1940. Lisbon 1957.
Réthy, Dr L. and Probszt, Dr G., *Corpus Nummorum Hungeriae*, reprint. Graz 1958.
Schembri, Canon H. Calleja, *Coins and Medals of the Knights of Malta*. London 1908.
Severin, H. M., *Gold and Platinum Coinage of Imperial Russia from 1701–1911*. New York 1958.
Schou, H. H., *Danske og Norske Mønter*. Copenhagen 1926.
Schulman, J., *Nederlandsche Munten van 1795–1945*. Amsterdam 1946.
Testa, G. S., *Ducatoni, Piastre, Scudi, Talleri e Loro Multipli*, Vol. I. Casa Savoia. Rome 1951. Vol. II. Romani Pontefici. Rome 1952.
Yriarte, José de, *Catalogo de los Reales de A Ocho Espanoles*. Madrid 1955.

Index

ACKEY, the, 136–7
Aegina, 31
AE 38
Aes, 34
Africa, North, 132–5
  French West, 138
  British East, 139
Aimer, Philip, 75
Akbar I, 145
Albums, coin, 21
Alexander the Great, 33–4
Anna, the, 147 ff.
Angel d'or, 47
  English, 80, 81, 85
Antoninianus, the, 37, 66
Antoninus Pius, 39
Antony, Mark, 36–7
As, the, 34, 36, 37
Asia, British colonies in, 149
Ataturk, Kemal, 134
Athens, ancient, 31–2
Auctions, 16
Augustus, 37–8
Aureus, the, 37, 38
Australia, 154–6
Austria, 54–5

BAIBAR, Mamluk, 134
Baltimore, Lord (1652), 105
Barbarous radiates, 67
Barcelona, 57
Baronail issues, 75
Becker, Carl, 27
Belgium, 58
Bellovacian coins, 65
Blondeau, Pierre, 90
Bolivar, Simon, 128
Bonaparte, Joseph, 57
  Louis, 57–8
Boulton, Matthew, 94
Bracteates, 50
Brenner, Victor D., 114
Briot, Nicholas, 48, 88
Broad, the, 89
Brugsal, Alexander of, 82
Brunswick-Lüneburg, 52
Byzantium, 41

CABINETS, coin, 21–2
Caesar, Julius, 36
Calpurnia, 35
Carolingians, the, 42
Carthage, 132–3
Cash, the, 150
Casts, plaster, making, 23
Cellini, Benvenuto, 56
Cent, the, U.S.A., 112–14
  Canada, 119
Centavo, the, 142
Central America, 123–9
Ceylon, 147–9
Charlemagne, 42
China, 149–51
Civil war (English), 88–9
Cleaning coins, 19–20
Cleopatra, 132
Clubs, numismatic, 22
Cnossos, 32–3
Coining, techniques of, 24–7
Collecting, specialization in, 13–15
  purchasing for, 15–16
  condition of coins, 17–18
  rarity and value, 18
  cleaning, 19–20
  housing, 21–2
  clubs and societies, 22
  photography and rubbing, 22–3
Commonwealth (1649–53), 89
Condition, rating of, 17–18
Congo, the, 138–9
Constantine, 40
Constantius, 66–7
Corinth, 32
Croeseus, 29
Crown, the, 83 ff., 156, 157
Cyrenaica, 32

DALER, the, 61
Danegeld, 60, 70
Dealers, value of, 16–17
Denar, the, 49–50
Denarius, the, 35–6, 37, 38
Deniers, Canadian, 117
  French, 42, 47
  Polish, 59

INDEX

Dengi, the, 63
Denmark, 61–2
Dime, the, 114
Diocletian, 38
Directory, the, 49
Dirhem, the, 144
Dollar, American, 104, 112, 115
  Bank of England, 95
  Canadian, 121
  East India Company, 145
  holey, 117, 154
  rix, 149
  West Indian, 130
Drachm, denominations of, 51–2
Ducat, the, Dutch, 58
  Polish, 59
  Russian, 63–4
  Venetian, 55
Dupondius, the, 37, 66
Dupré, William, 48

EAGLE, the, 115
East Africa, British, 139
  German, 142
East India Company, 145–9
Ecu, the, 47, 48
Egypt, 132–3, 134–5
Eire, 103
Electrum, 30
Endybis, King, 135
England: Early Britain, 65–72
  Norman, 72–5
  Plantagenet, 75–81
  Tudor, 82–7
  Stuart, 87–92
  Hanoverian, 93–8
  Windsor, 98–9
Equatorial Africa, 138
Escudo, the, 142
Esterlings, 77
Ethiopia, 135–6
Euainetos, 32

FARTHING, the, 77 ff.
Feuchtwanger, Lewis, 114
Fifty-shilling, 89
Fiji, 158
Fiorino, the, 56, 76
Florence, 55–6
Florin, the, 78, 97, 155, 157
Flying eagle cents, 113
Follis, the, 38, 67
Forgery, methods of, 26–8
Formosa, 151

Franc, the, 49
France, 42–9
Fugio cents, 112
Fyrk, the, 61

GEORGE-NOBLE, the, 83
Germany, 49–53
Ghana, 137–8
Godless florin, 97
Gold Coast, 136–7
Gold-gulden, the, 50
Gothic crown, 97
Graumann, J. P., 52
Gray, Kruger, 157
Greece, ancient, 29–34
Groat, the, 76–7, 80–6, 157
Gros, the, 59
Gros tournois, 47
Groschen, the, 50
Groze, the, 60
Guadeloupe, 131
Guinea denominations, 90, 94
Gulden, the, 58
Gun money, 91, 103
Gunthamund, 133
Gyllen, the, 61

HADLEIE, Robert de, 77
Haile Selassie, Emperor, 136
Half cent, 113
Half dollar, 115–16
Half-crown, the, 85 ff., 157
Halfdene, 69
Halfpenny, the, 69 ff., 157
Half groat, 87, 88
Haroun Er Rashid, 144
Hidalgo, 128
Hill, Sir George, 28
Hog money, 105
Holland, 57–8
  in Ceylon, 148
Hsueh-Tung, 150–1

ICHIBUBAN, the, 153
India, 144–7
Indian head cent, 113
Inlaid coins, 135
Inonu, Ismet, 134
Ireland, 102–3
Italy, 55–7
Iturbide, Augustin, 128

INDEX

JAMAICA, 130
Japan, 151-3
Judaea, 40

KAMIL, Hussein, 135
Key money, 135
'Kipper and Wipper', 51
Kopeck, the, 60, 63-4
Kruger, Paul, 141
Kuang Hsu, 150-1

LARIN, the, 148
Legionary coins, 66
Le Yuan Hung, 151
Lima coins, 93
Lincoln head cent, 113-14
Lire, the, 55
Lombardy, 55
Longinus, 35
Louis d'argent, 48
Luxembourg, 58
Lydia, 29-31

MACEDON, 33-4
Madagascar, 142-3
Maltravers farthings, 89
Mark, the, American, 112
   German, 53
   Swedish, 61
Martinique, 130-1
Maryland, 105
Massachusetts, 105
Matapane, the, 55
Maundy money, 90-1, 95
Medici, the, 56
Menelik II, 136
Merovingians, the, 42
Mestrelle, Eloye, 25, 86
Metapontum, 33
Metcalfe, Percy, 98, 157
Miliarense, the, 38
Mohur, the, 145, 146
Morelos, Don Jose, 127-8
Morocco, 134
Moulton, William, 111
Mozambique, 142

NEWBY, Mark, 105-6
Newfoundland, 121
New Guinea, 157-8
New Zealand, 156-7
Nezana, King, 136
Nickel, 114
Nigeria, 137-8

Noble, the, 78-80
Norway, 62
Nova constellatio, 112

OBAN, the, 152
Obol, the, 32
Obole, the, 42, 47
Octavian, *see* Augustus
Offa, 68
Öre, the, 61
Örtugo, the, 61

PAGODA, the, 146
Papacy, the, 56-7
Parisis d'or, 47
Parthia, 144

Pavillon d'or, 47
Persia, 33
Penning, the, 60
Penningar, the, 61
Penny, English, 68 ff., 157
   Scandinavian, 60
Pfennig, the, 49-50
Philip of Macedon, 33
Photography of coins, 22-3
Piastre, the, 135
Pice, the, 147
Pieces of eight, 104, 126
Piefor de la Chaise, 47
Pilate, Pontius, 40
Platinum, 64
Poland, 58-60
Pompey, 36-7
Pond, the, 141
Portcullis coins, 145-6
Pound, the, 85 ff.
Preservation, rating of, 17-18
Prussia, 51
Ptolemy I, 132

QUADRANS, the, 37
Quarter, U.S., 115
Quinarius, the, 36, 37, 66
Quint, the, 112

RARITY, degrees of, 18
Ready, Robert, 27
Reales, 125, 130, 154
Restrikes, 27-8
Rhodesias, the, 139-40
Riebeeck, Jan van, 141

INDEX

Rijksdaaler, the, 58, 61
Rin, the, 153
Rome, classical, 34–41
  in Britain, 66
  in North Africa, 132–3
Rouble, the, 60, 62–4
Rubbings, making, 23
Rupee, East African, 139, 142
  Indian, 145 ff.
  Sinhalese, 148–9
Russia, 62–4
  over Poland, 59–60
Ryal, the, 80

SAXONY, 50–1, 59
Scandinavia, 60–2
Sceat, the, 42, 67
Scotland, 100–2
Scudo, the, 56
Sede vacante, coins, 56–7
Semis, the, 37
Semissis, the, 38
Sen, the, 152 ff.
Sestertius, the, 36, 37
Shekel, the, 40
Shilling, the, 84 ff., 155, 157
  North American, 105
Short-cross coinage, 75–6
Sierra Leone, 137–8
Simnel, Lambert, 102
Sixpence, 85 ff., 155, 157
Societies, numismatic, 22
Solidus, the, 38, 42
Sol, the, 117
Somalia, 142
Somalo, the, 142
South Africa, 140–1
Sovereign, the, 82 ff., 155
Spade guineas, 94
Spain, 57
Speciedaler, the, 61, 62
Stater, the, 33
  British copies, 65
Stiver, the, 149
St Lucia, 131
St Patrick's halfpence, 105
Sudan, 135
Sun Yat Sen, 151
Sweden, 61
Syracuse, 32

TAEL, the, 151
Takoe, the, 137
Taler, the, 50–4
Talarus, the, 55
Tanga, the, 148
Tealby coinage, 75
Tenpo Tsuho, the, 153
Tepuzque, the, 124–5
Testerne, the, 146
Testoons, 48, 82, 83
Thrace, 32
Three-farthings, 86
Threehalfpence, 86
Threepence, 86, 88, 105, 157
Tiberius, 39
Tokens, American, 111
  Australian, 154–7
  Canadian, 118–19
  English, 86–7, 90
Tortola, 131
Trajan, 39
Tremissis, the, 38, 67
Tribute penny, 40
Tunis, 134
Turkey, 133–5
Twopence, 89

VALUE OF COINS, 18
Venice, 55
Vigo coins, 92
Vespasian, 38

WA-DO, 152
Wampum, 104
Warin, Jean, 48
Washington, George, 113
Watt, James, 94
Weight standards, Greek, 30–1
Wendenpfenige, 59
West Africa, British, 137–8
  French, 138
Wood, William, 106, 111

YEN, the, 153
Yuan Shi Kai, 151

ZLOTE, the, 60